TABLE OF CONTENTS ◆ PRACTICE

MW00338894

Math Explorations and Applications Level 4

TABLE OF CONTENTS ◆ PRACTICE (Continued)

PRACTICE

Name_____

A rack in the gym at Richard's school holds tennis balls. It is partially covered so that you cannot count the exact number of balls in the rack. Estimate the total number of balls in the rack.

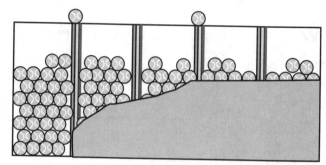

❶ Write your best estimate of how many balls there are.

_____

❷ Richard's friends helped him carry away some balls. Five children took five balls each. How many balls did they take? Make a second estimate of how many balls there were.

_____

_____

❸ Five more children came. They each took five balls. So far ten children have taken five balls each. How many balls is that? Make a third estimate of how many balls there were.

_____

_____

❹ More children came and took balls. So far, 15 children have taken five balls each. How many balls have they taken? Make a fourth estimate of how many balls there were.

_____

_____

❺ All 15 children came back. They each took another five balls. Counting both times the children took some balls, how many balls did each child take?

_____

❻ How many balls have the 15 children taken all together?

_____

❼ There are now two balls left in the rack. Make a fifth estimate of how many balls there were all together.

_____

Write the numbers in standard form.

1. 70 + 6 _____

2. 300 + 40 + 7 _____

3. 900 + 90 + 9 _____

4. 2000 + 600 + 4 _____

5. 20,000 + 5000 + 300 _____

6. 5000 + 60 _____

7. 1 + 80 + 400 _____

8. 200,000 + 2000 + 2 _____

9. 8,000,000 + 400 + 3 _____

10. 7 + 60 + 900 + 7000 _____

11. 100 + 3000 + 60,000 _____

12. 70,000,000 + 50,000 _____

13. 40 + 9000 + 70,000 _____

14. 10,000 + 4 _____

15. 8000 + 800 + 80 + 8 _____

16. 8000 + 700 + 80 + 8 _____

17. 8000 + 800 + 80 + 7 _____

18. 30 + 3000 + 7 _____

Count up. Write the missing numbers.

1 3, 4, _____, _____, _____, 8, 9, _____, _____, 12, 13, 14, 15, _____, 17

2 284, 285, 286, _____, _____, _____, 290, 291, 292, 293, 294

3 4667, 4668, 4669, _____, _____, _____, 4673, 4674, 4675

4 7298, _____, _____, 7301, 7302, 7303, 7304, 7305, 7306

5 62,452; 62,453; 62,454; _____; _____; _____; 62,458

Count down. Write the missing numbers.

6 18, 17, 16, _____, _____, _____, 12, 11, _____, _____, 8, 7, _____, 5

7 34, 33, 32, 31, _____, _____, _____, _____, 26, 25, 24, 23, 22

8 744, 743, 742, 741, 740, 739, _____, _____, 736

9 504, 503, 502, 501, _____, _____, _____, _____, 496

10 6603, _____, _____, _____, 6599, 6598, 6597, 6596

Count up or down. Write the missing numbers.

11 707, 708, 709, _____, _____, _____, 713, 714, 715, 716, 717

12 418, 417, 416, 415, 414, 413, 412, 411, _____, _____, 408

13 1014, 1015, 1016, 1017, 1018, 1019, _____, _____, 1022

14 1004, 1003, 1002, _____, _____, _____, 998, 997, 996, 995

15 3097, 3098, 3099, _____, _____, _____, 3103, 3104, 3105

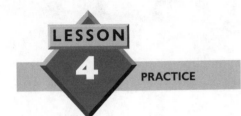

Name_____

Complete the chart. Use each digit once.

	Use These Digits	Greatest Number	Least Number
1	7, 1, 2		
2	8, 7		
3	4, 9		
4	2, 6, 1		
5	9, 2, 2		
6	4, 5, 5		
7	5, 1, 7, 8		
8	8, 4, 8, 4		
9	2, 5, 1, 1, 4		
10	6, 2, 2, 7, 7		

Write six different numbers in order from greatest to least.

11 Use the digits 6, 7, and 8. _____

12 Use the digits 1, 5, and 7. _____

13 Use the digits 2, 9, and 4. _____

14 Use the digits 2, 6, and 5. _____

15 Use the digits 7, 3, and 6. _____

Name_____

Are You Shiny or Rusty?
Very shiny   43 or more right
Shiny   38–42 right
A bit rusty   33–37 right
Rusty   Fewer than 33 right

Add.

1 7 + 2 = _____   **2** _____ = 5 + 9   **3** _____ = 2 + 1   **4** 6 + 4 = _____

5 _____ = 4 + 2   **6** 6 + 6 = _____   **7** 8 + 2 = _____   **8** 7 + 5 = _____

9 6 + 4 = _____   **10** 8 + 5 = _____   **11** _____ = 4 + 5   **12** 7 + 3 = _____

13 6 + 5 = _____   **14** 9 + 8 = _____   **15** 0 + 4 = _____   **16** _____ = 1 + 7

17 9 + 1 = _____   **18** 4 + 8 = _____   **19** 4 + 4 = _____   **20** 0 + 6 = _____

21 _____ = 7 + 3   **22** 9 + 6 = _____   **23** 8 + 3 = _____   **24** _____ = 5 + 5

25 2 + 7 = _____   **26** 8 + 8 = _____   **27** _____ = 3 + 5   **28** 5 + 6 = _____

29 3 + 9 = _____   **30** _____ = 7 + 7   **31** _____ = 6 + 3   **32** 9 + 9 = _____

33 8 + 4	**34** 9 + 1	**35** 6 + 7	**36** 5 + 5	**37** 2 + 4	**38** 4 + 3
39 7 6 + 3	**40** 2 5 + 6	**41** 4 0 + 5	**42** 6 6 + 7	**43** 5 3 + 8	**44** 3 3 + 3

45 7 + 2 + 2 + 2 + 3 = _____   **46** 2 + 2 + 2 + 2 + 2 = _____

47 6 + 2 + 4 + 5 + 4 = _____   **48** 2 + 3 + 4 + 5 + 6 = _____

Are You Shiny or Rusty?

Very shiny	47 or more right
Shiny	42–46 right
A bit rusty	37–41 right
Rusty	Fewer than 37 right

Subtract.

1 7 – 2 = _____ **2** _____ = 12 – 8 **3** 2 – 1 = _____ **4** 6 – 4 = _____

5 _____ = 4 – 2 **6** 10 – 6 = _____ **7** 11 – 4 = _____ **8** 7 – 0 = _____

9 6 – 6 = _____ **10** 9 – 2 = _____ **11** _____ = 5 – 2 **12** 14 – 6 = _____

13 13 – 5 = _____ **14** 9 – 8 = _____ **15** 10 – 8 = _____ **16** _____ = 6 – 1

17 9 – 1 = _____ **18** 8 – 5 = _____ **19** 4 – 4 = _____ **20** 6 – 0 = _____

21 _____ = 7 – 3 **22** 19 – 9 = _____ **23** 8 – 3 = _____ **24** _____ = 11 – 5

25 7 – 5 = _____ **26** 17 – 8 = _____ **27** _____ = 15 – 7 **28** 5 – 5 = _____

29 15 – 9 = _____ **30** _____ = 8 – 7 **31** _____ = 16 – 8 **32** 6 – 1 = _____

33 8 – 4

34 9 – 1

35 10 – 7

36 6 – 5

37 4 – 4

38 7 – 3

39 12 – 6

40 14 – 5

41 9 – 7

42 11 – 5

43 4 – 3

44 9 – 6

45 7 – 2

46 14 – 4

47 8 – 0

48 12 – 9

49 15 – 6

50 9 – 4

51 13 – 4

52 9 – 9

Name_____

Are You Shiny or Rusty?

Very shiny   43 or more right
Shiny   38–42 right
A bit rusty   33–37 right
Rusty   Fewer than 33 right

Add or subtract.

1 $2 + 7 =$ _____   **2** $6 - 4 =$ _____   **3** $7 - 5 =$ _____   **4** $7 - 4 =$ _____

5 $8 + 8 =$ _____   **6** $7 + 7 =$ _____   **7** $9 - 8 =$ _____   **8** _____ $= 3 + 6$

9 _____ $= 10 - 6$ **10** $9 + 6 =$ _____   **11** $2 + 0 =$ _____   **12** $0 + 0 =$ _____

13 _____ $= 7 + 1$ **14** _____ $= 5 - 3$ **15** _____ $= 10 - 9$ **16** $9 + 5 =$ _____

17 $3 + 7 =$ _____   **18** $9 - 1 =$ _____   **19** $6 - 5 =$ _____   **20** $6 + 7 =$ _____

21 $4 - 3 =$ _____   **22** $10 + 4 =$ _____   **23** _____ $= 10 + 9$ **24** $5 + 4 =$ _____

25 $6 + 4 =$ _____   **26** $7 + 5 =$ _____   **27** $3 + 3 =$ _____   **28** $7 - 6 =$ _____

29 $\begin{array}{r} 7 \\ - 3 \\ \hline \end{array}$ **30** $\begin{array}{r} 5 \\ + 5 \\ \hline \end{array}$ **31** $\begin{array}{r} 9 \\ - 6 \\ \hline \end{array}$ **32** $\begin{array}{r} 9 \\ + 9 \\ \hline \end{array}$ **33** $\begin{array}{r} 10 \\ + 5 \\ \hline \end{array}$

34 $\begin{array}{r} 10 \\ - 5 \\ \hline \end{array}$ **35** $\begin{array}{r} 9 \\ - 7 \\ \hline \end{array}$ **36** $\begin{array}{r} 10 \\ + 10 \\ \hline \end{array}$ **37** $\begin{array}{r} 9 \\ + 1 \\ \hline \end{array}$ **38** $\begin{array}{r} 9 \\ + 7 \\ \hline \end{array}$

39 $\begin{array}{r} 8 \\ - 7 \\ \hline \end{array}$ **40** $\begin{array}{r} 6 \\ - 2 \\ \hline \end{array}$ **41** $\begin{array}{r} 10 \\ - 3 \\ \hline \end{array}$ **42** $\begin{array}{r} 8 \\ + 7 \\ \hline \end{array}$ **43** $\begin{array}{r} 4 \\ + 4 \\ \hline \end{array}$

44 $\begin{array}{r} 7 \\ + 2 \\ \hline \end{array}$ **45** $\begin{array}{r} 2 \\ + 5 \\ \hline \end{array}$ **46** $\begin{array}{r} 8 \\ - 6 \\ \hline \end{array}$ **47** $\begin{array}{r} 4 \\ + 7 \\ \hline \end{array}$ **48** $\begin{array}{r} 10 \\ - 10 \\ \hline \end{array}$

Name_____

Complete each chart. Watch the function rule.

1 (−3)

In	Out
18	15
15	12
12	9
9	
6	
3	

2 (+4)

In	Out
0	4
1	
2	
3	
4	
5	

3 (−8)

In	Out
18	
16	
14	
12	
10	
8	

4 (+6)

In	Out
3	
5	
7	
9	
11	
13	

5 (−10)

In	Out
90	
80	
70	
60	
50	
40	

6 (−2)

In	Out
19	
16	
13	
10	
7	
4	

Solve these problems.

1 David has $16. If he buys a baseball for $4, how much money will he have left?

_____

2 Jan bought 12 cookies. She ate some and now has seven cookies left. How many cookies did she eat?

_____

3 Alan runs 20 kilometers every week. So far this week he has run 12 kilometers. How many more kilometers does he need to run this week?

_____

4 There were nine posters on Emiko's wall, but some fell off. There are seven posters left on the wall. How many fell off?

_____

5 Chris gave away five baseball cards. She has seven left. How many cards did she start with?

_____

6 Bill had six crayons. He found some more. How many does he have now?

_____

7 Carlos needs to collect 16 tree leaves for a display. So far he has collected six leaves. How many more leaves does he need?

_____

8 Nancy has 10¢. She wants to buy a pencil that costs 15¢. How much more money does she need?

_____

9 If Luisa had ten peaches and ate three, how many would she have left?

_____

10 There were 15 problems on a math quiz. Keith missed two. How many problems did he get right?

_____

Name_____

Find the perimeter.

1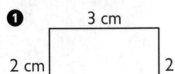

3 cm

2 cm   2 cm

3 cm

_____

2

4 cm

4 cm   4 cm

4 cm

_____

3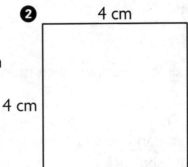

4 cm

3 cm   3 cm

4 cm

_____

4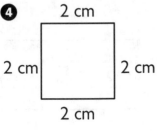

2 cm

2 cm   2 cm

2 cm

_____

5

2 cm

1 cm   1 cm

2 cm

_____

6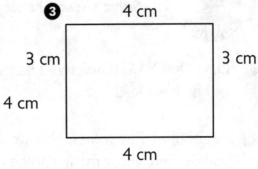

4 cm

4 cm   4 cm

4 cm   4 cm

_____

7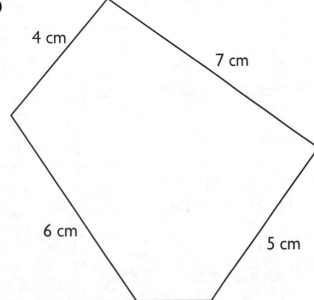

4 cm

7 cm

6 cm

5 cm

2 cm

_____

8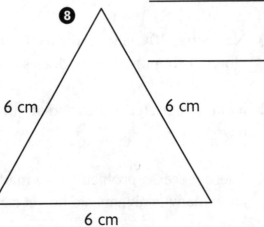

6 cm   6 cm

6 cm

_____

Study the chart. Then answer the questions for the zoos listed in the table.

Major Public Zoos in the United States

Zoo	Yearly Attendance	Acres	Number of Animal Species
Baltimore	600,000	180	1200
Brookfield	2,000,000	215	400
Los Angeles	1,400,000	80	440
Philadelphia	1,300,000	42	437
St. Louis	2,700,000	83	699
San Diego	3,000,000	125	800

1 Which zoo has the greatest attendance? _____

2 Does the zoo in problem 1 also have the greatest number of species of animals? _____

3 Which zoo has the least attendance? _____

4 Does the zoo in problem 3 also have the least number of acres? _____

5 Which two zoos have about the same number of acres?

_____

6 Which three zoos have about the same number of species of animals?

_____

7 Does any one zoo have all three—the least attendance, the least number of acres, and the least number of species of animals? _____

8 Does any one zoo have all three—the greatest attendance, the greatest number of acres, and the greatest number of species of animals? _____

Name_____

Add.

1   65
    + 23

2   27
    + 31

3   45
    + 45

4   86
    + 39

5   66
    + 66

6   48
    + 92

7   200
    + 37

8   600
    + 287

9   548
    + 273

10   805
    + 345

11   3872
    + 7954

12   74,315
    + 26,494

13   2,893,417
    + 6,484,385

14   27
      36
    + 45

15   216
      387
    + 691

16   305
      165
      425
    + 95

17   903
      769
      542
    + 281

18   207
      711
      491
    + 355

19   576
      143
      278
    + 685

20   473
      221
      852
    + 315

21   370
      825
      564
    + 231

22   428
      917
      666
    + 190

23   783
      216
      405
    + 504

24   113
      332
      810
    + 275

25   702
      636
      470
    + 173

Name_____

Subtract.

❶   74
    − 23

❷   88
    − 80

❸   92
    − 37

❹   71
    − 69

❺   44
    − 39

❻   683
    − 421

❼   745
    − 227

❽   304
    − 178

❾   120
    − 88

❿   708
    − 224

⓫   900
    − 43

⓬   500
    − 429

⓭   400
    − 172

⓮   800
    − 355

⓯   304
    − 267

⓰   5000
    −   3

⓱   6453
    − 2001

⓲   1783
    − 599

⓳   4865
    − 1037

⓴   860
    − 243

㉑   440
    − 284

㉒   807
    − 359

㉓   610
    − 247

㉔   1700
    − 408

㉕   4,567,983
    − 2,743,697

㉖   641
    − 293

㉗   784
    − 652

㉘   2976
    − 1849

㉙   2194
    − 1999

㉚   2,763,471
    − 1,092,343

Name_____

Add or subtract. Use shortcuts when you can.

1
```
   42
+  47
```

2
```
   77
−  24
```

3
```
   86
+  44
```

4
```
   90
−   5
```

5
```
   99
+   7
```

6
```
   575
+  125
```

7
```
   410
+   97
```

8
```
   350
+  125
```

9
```
   425
−   75
```

10
```
   684
+  116
```

11
```
   5457
+  3002
```

12
```
   1762
−   702
```

13
```
   356
+  121
```

14
```
   798
−  208
```

15
```
   321
+  475
```

16
```
   698
+  102
```

17
```
   1800
+   212
```

18
```
   958
−  107
```

19
```
   880
−  220
```

20
```
   550
+  160
```

21
```
   2673
−  1492
```

22
```
   649
+  281
```

23
```
   1482
+  1641
```

24
```
   1700
−  1251
```

25
```
   1642
+  1999
```

26
```
   5500
−  3400
```

27
```
   15,678
−  14,556
```

28
```
   1800
−  750
```

29
```
   1593
+  1621
```

30
```
   750,000
+  250,000
```

Patty made a chart to help her find the least expensive store. First she decided which brands and products she wanted, then she recorded their prices. Complete the bottom line of Patty's chart.

Item	Price		
	Larry's Mart	More for Less	Best Mart
Shiny Shampoo (travel size)	89¢	78¢	85¢
Bath Powder (travel size)	85¢	95¢	92¢
Best Toothpaste (travel size)	69¢	75¢	72¢
Total			

1 Which store is least expensive for the three items listed? _____

2 Which store is most expensive? _____

3 For each store write the total amount in dollars and cents. _____

4 Patty met Mrs. O'Leary, who was going shopping. "I have to buy soap, hair conditioner, bath tissue, and paper towels," said Mrs. O'Leary. "Do you know which store will be most expensive?" she asked. Does Patty know the answer to Mrs. O'Leary's question? Why or why not?

_____

_____

What is the right sign? Draw <, >, or =.

1 32 ◯ 27

2 42 ◯ 52

3 84 ◯ 88

4 104 ◯ 401

5 768 ◯ 678

6 6 + 7 ◯ 23

7 12 ◯ 11 + 11

8 105 ◯ 100 – 5

9 58 ◯ 62 + 8

10 84 ◯ 70 + 9

11 100 ◯ 100 + 50

12 200 ◯ 127 + 139

13 67 – 18 ◯ 20

14 72 ◯ 70 + 20

15 38 ◯ 41 + 27

16 66 ◯ 66 – 6

17 70 + 1 ◯ 68

18 16 + 16 ◯ 116

19 2 + 3 ◯ 4 + 3

20 16 + 7 ◯ 7 + 16

21 16 – 7 ◯ 16 + 7

22 50 + 20 ◯ 20 + 50

23 50 + 20 ◯ 50 – 20

24 27 + 6 ◯ 17 + 3

25 48 – 20 ◯ 32 – 20

26 58 + 7 ◯ 54 + 4

27 27 – 4 ◯ 21 – 3

28 86 – 18 ◯ 50 – 25

29 105 – 28 ◯ 125 – 18

30 47 + 39 ◯ 39 + 47

31 64 – 16 ◯ 39 + 42

32 84 – 29 ◯ 62 + 10

Choose the correct answer. Discuss your methods.

1   76
   + 2☐

  a. 90
  b. 100
  c. 110

2   302
   + ☐9

  a. 381
  b. 481
  c. 1011

3   626
   + 5☐0

  a. 146
  b. 1056
  c. 1146

4   275
   + ☐4

  a. 99
  b. 199
  c. 299

5   41☐
   + 1☐

  a. 375
  b. 425
  c. 525

6   83☐
   + 79

  a. 809
  b. 917
  c. 1009

7   2☐☐
   + 424

  a. 90
  b. 700
  c. 900

8   35☐
   + 1☐9

  a. 420
  b. 530
  c. 600

9   7☐0
   + 125

  a. 845
  b. 948
  c. 1045

10   98
   − 3☐

  a. 64
  b. 72
  c. 94

11   7☐
   − 56

  a. 9
  b. 19
  c. 29

12   746
   − 40☐

  a. 137
  b. 237
  c. 337

13   3☐4
   − 122

  a. 182
  b. 282
  c. 420

14   71☐
   − 53☐

  a. 95
  b. 185
  c. 225

15   2☐☐8
   − 809

  a. 669
  b. 769
  c. 1869

16   4☐5☐
   − 739

  a. 4911
  b. 3919
  c. 3809

Name_____

SOCIAL STUDIES CONNECTION

Sometimes you don't need an exact answer. Select the best answer for each problem. You don't have to do the calculations.

1 Jamestown, Virginia, was established in 1607. About how many years ago was that?

   a. About 400   **b.** About 40   **c.** About 140   _____

2 France recognized America's independence in 1778. About how many years ago was that?

   a. About 20   **b.** About 200   **c.** About 50   _____

3 The United States of America negotiated the Louisiana Purchase from France in 1803. About how many years ago was that?

   a. About 100   **b.** About 20   **c.** About 200   _____

4 X rays were discovered by German physicist Wilhelm Roentgen in 1895. About how many years ago was that?

   a. About 100   **b.** About 10   **c.** About 50   _____

5 In 1990 the population of Kansas City, Missouri, was 435,146, and the population of Memphis, Tennessee, was 610,337. About how many more people lived in Memphis than in Kansas City?

   a. About 175,000   **b.** About 1,750,000   **c.** About 17,500   _____

6 In 1990 the population of Dallas, Texas, was 1,006,877, and the population of Indianapolis, Indiana, was 741,952. About how many more people lived in Dallas than in Indianapolis?

   a. About 2500   **b.** About 25,000   **c.** About 250,000   _____

7 The air distance between Chicago, Illinois, and Salt Lake City, Utah, is 1260 miles. The air distance between Chicago and San Francisco, California, is 1858 miles. Chicago is about how much farther from San Francisco than it is from Salt Lake City?

   a. About 60 miles   **b.** About 600 miles   **c.** About 6 miles   _____

Name_____

Add or subtract with and without your calculator. See if you get the same answer both ways.

1 $3 - 1 - 1 - 1 =$ _0_

2 $30 - 10 - 10 =$ _10_

3 $100 + 60 =$ _160_

4 $70 - 10 =$ _60_

5 $80 - 12 =$ _68_

6 $100 + 90 =$ _190_

7 $60 - 2 =$ _58_

8 $40 + 20 =$ _60_

9 $15 - 6 =$ _9_

10 $100 + 36 =$ _64_

11 $150 - 50 =$ _100_

12 $7 + 7 =$ _14_

13 $9 - 9 =$ _0_

14 $90 - 90 =$ _0_

15 $773 + 87 =$ _860_

16 $773 - 87 =$ _686_

17 $683 - 80 =$ _603_

18 $603 + 80 =$ _683_

19 $8 + 5 =$ _13_

20 $80 + 50 =$ _130_

21 $800 + 500 =$ _1300_

22 $8 - 6 =$ _2_

23 $80 - 60 =$ _20_

24 $800 - 600 =$ _200_

25 $48 + 503 =$ _551_

26 $48 + 53 =$ _101_

27 $480 + 530 =$ _1010_

28 $650 - 51 =$ _599_

29 $409 + 200 =$ _609_

30 $429 - 20 =$ _409_

Figure out how to change the first display to the second display. Try to use no more than one step.

31 0.   82. _____

32 543.   43. _____

33 36.   836. _____

34 800.   0. _____

35 5.   100. _____

Name_____

Choose the correct answer.

1 About how much of the square is shaded?

a. $\frac{1}{4}$　　b. $\frac{1}{2}$　　c. $\frac{2}{3}$

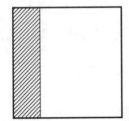

2 About how full is the fuel tank?

 a. $\frac{3}{4}$　　b. $\frac{1}{4}$　　c. $\frac{1}{2}$

3 About how much of the cake is left?

a. $\frac{1}{2}$　　b. $\frac{2}{3}$　　c. $\frac{1}{5}$

4 The length of the short pipe is about what fraction of the length of the long pipe?

a. $\frac{1}{4}$　　b. $\frac{1}{2}$　　c. $\frac{2}{3}$

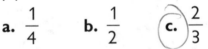

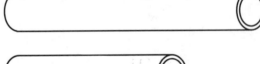

5 About how full is the glass?

a. $\frac{4}{5}$　　b. $\frac{2}{5}$　　c. $\frac{1}{5}$

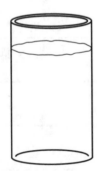

6 About how much of the yard has not been mowed?

a. $\frac{1}{3}$　　b. $\frac{1}{4}$　　c. $\frac{3}{4}$

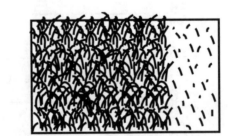

Name_____

Solve these problems.

1 Heather cut her birthday cake into 12 equal pieces. Then eight pieces were eaten. Is more than $\frac{1}{2}$ of the cake left? _____

2 At Mark's school, $\frac{3}{4}$ of the teachers are women. Are there more women teachers than men teachers at Mark's school? _____

3 A sweater usually sells for $10. It is on sale for $8. Is that more than $\frac{1}{4}$ off the regular price? _____

4 Last week Peter started knitting a scarf that will have 16 identical sections. He has knitted six sections so far. Is the scarf more than $\frac{1}{2}$ finished yet? _____

5 A bicycle costs $75. Rosa is saving money to buy it. She has saved $29. Has she saved more than $\frac{1}{3}$ of the cost of the bicycle yet? _____

6 Mr. Wong is driving to the beach, which is 100 kilometers from his house. He has 60 kilometers left to go. Is he more than halfway there? _____

7 Brenda is baking cookies. The recipe calls for 1000 grams of sugar and 1800 grams of flour. Because Brenda has only 500 grams of sugar, she can make only $\frac{1}{2}$ of the recipe. How many grams of flour should she use? _____

8 The gas tank of Mrs. Jensen's car holds 40 liters. She just put in 29 liters of gas to fill the tank. About how full was the tank before the gas was added? _____

a. About $\frac{1}{4}$ full   **b.** About $\frac{1}{2}$ full   **c.** About $\frac{3}{4}$ full

Write the amount in dollars and cents. Watch your numbering.

1 15 cents _____

2 3 dimes _____

3 5 nickels and 1 dime _____

4 5 dimes and 4 cents _____

5 6 cents _____

6 4 dimes and 7 cents _____

7 7 nickels _____

8 1 quarter and 1 dime _____

9 3 dimes, 2 nickels, and 3 cents _____

10 1 dollar and 2 dimes _____

11 1 dollar and 4 nickels _____

12 2 dollars and 8 dimes _____

13 1 dollar, 2 quarters, and 2 dimes _____

14 1 dollar, 1 dime, and 2 cents _____

15 1 dollar, 1 nickel, and 7 cents _____

16 3 dollars and 3 quarters _____

17 2 dollars and 7 dimes _____

18 5 dollars, 2 dimes, and 2 cents _____

19 4 dollars and 1 cent _____

20 3 dollars, 2 quarters, and 6 cents _____

What is the right sign? Draw <, >, or =.

21 $5.00 $\bigcirc$ $4.49

22 $60.40 $\bigcirc$ $6.04

23 $22.22 $\bigcirc$ $2.22

24 $35 $\bigcirc$ $35.00

25 $86.00 $\bigcirc$ $86

26 $0.24 $\bigcirc$ $2.40

27 $0.05 $\bigcirc$ $5.05

28 $42.00 $\bigcirc$ $42

29 $0.97 $\bigcirc$ $97

30 $5.99 $\bigcirc$ $5.19

31 $15 $\bigcirc$ $15.00

32 $0.67 $\bigcirc$ $6.70

In each problem two of the answers are clearly wrong and one is correct. Choose the correct answer.

1 $6.20 + $3.10 = _____   **a.** $7.40   **b.** $9.30   **c.** $3.10

2 $0.98 − $0.61 = _____   **a.** $1.59   **b.** $1.49   **c.** $0.37

3 $5.40 + $3.60 = _____   **a.** $8.00   **b.** $1.80   **c.** $9.00

4 $9.05 − $6.30 = _____   **a.** $2.75   **b.** $15.35   **c.** $3.75

5 $0.47 + $0.86 = _____   **a.** $2.00   **b.** $1.33   **c.** $1.42

6 $2.75 − $1.50 = _____   **a.** $0.75   **b.** $1.25   **c.** $4.25

7 $4.98 + $1.79 = _____   **a.** $5.48   **b.** $6.77   **c.** $1.97

8 $0.75 + $3.25 = _____   **a.** $5.00   **b.** $2.29   **c.** $4.00

9 $8.15 + $2.15 = _____   **a.** $6.00   **b.** $10.30   **c.** $9.25

10 $1.98 + $0.49 = _____   **a.** $1.37   **b.** $1.49   **c.** $2.47

11 $8.00 − $6.50 = _____   **a.** $2.50   **b.** $14.50   **c.** $1.50

12 $6.98 + $2.39 = _____   **a.** $9.37   **b.** $4.02   **c.** $8.56

13 $4.86 − $0.59 = _____   **a.** $4.65   **b.** $3.37   **c.** $4.27

14 $7.98 + $3.98 = _____   **a.** $4.00   **b.** $10.96   **c.** $11.96

15 $6.25 + $1.75 = _____   **a.** $8.00   **b.** $7.50   **c.** $4.25

16 $10.00 − $2.47 = _____   **a.** $8.53   **b.** $7.53   **c.** $7.63

 Solve these problems.

17 William has $5.00. He wants to buy a ball that costs $8.15. There is a tax of 41 cents. How much more money must he save? _____

18 At the store the bill came to $32.39. Rhonda gave the clerk two 20-dollar bills. How much change should she get? _____

Name_____

MEDIUM CHEESE PIZZA $6.00		
MEAT TOPPINGS	**VEGETABLE TOPPINGS**	**DRINKS**
pepperoni–90¢	mushrooms–45¢	cola–80¢
sausage–85¢	green peppers–40¢	root beer–90¢
hamburger–80¢	olives–50¢	lemon-lime–75¢
ham–75¢	onions–35¢	

A. J. budgets $8.00 per week to spend on a pizza meal. He wants to always get one meat topping, one vegetable topping, and a drink. Help A. J. plan some meals.

Complete the chart.

Week	Meat	Vegetable	Drink	Total Price
1. $6.00 +	pepperoni, 90¢	onions, 35¢	lemon-lime, 75¢	$8.00
2.	sausage, 85¢			
3.				
4.				

Use the menu to answer these questions.

❶ Assume that A. J. still can spend only $8.00 and that he always orders one pizza with one meat topping, one vegetable topping, and one drink. What is the least expensive meal A. J. could have?

_____

❷ A. J. gets some extra money for his birthday so he decides to order a medium pizza with everything on it. How much will the pizza cost (without any drink)?

_____

Name_____

The store manager made a chart of the number of shirts sold during one week at his store. The bottom of the chart was accidentally torn off. Study what is left of his chart.

Day	Number of Shirts Sold
Monday	35
Tuesday	33
Wednesday	30
Thursday	32
Friday	35

Give exact answers to the questions below.

1 How many shirts were sold on

   a. Tuesday? _____

   b. Thursday? _____

2 On which day were exactly 30 shirts sold? _____

3 On which two days were the same number of shirts sold? _____

4 How many more shirts were sold on Friday than on Wednesday? _____

Estimate the answers to these questions.

5 About how many shirts will be sold on Saturday? _____

6 If the store is closed on Sunday, about how many shirts were sold during the entire week? _____

7 The store manager decided to hold a sale and stay open longer on Saturday. He sold at least as many shirts on Saturday as he did on Tuesday and Wednesday combined. About how many shirts did he sell on Saturday? _____

8 Make up three questions that can be answered from the chart. Ask a friend to answer your questions.

_____

_____

_____

Name_____

Count up or down. Write the missing numbers.

1 755, 756, _757_, _758_, _759_, _760_, _761_, 762

2 15,628; 15,627; 15,626; _15,625_; _15,624_; _15,623_; _15,622_; _15,621_; 15,620

Add or subtract to solve for *n*.

3 $15 - 7 = n$ _8_

4 $n = 8 + 7$ _15_

5 $n = 10 - 6$ _4_

6 $16 - 8 = n$ _8_

7 $4 + 9 = n$ _13_

8 $n = 6 + 5$ _11_

Solve for *n*.

9 $8 = 16 - n$ _8_

10 $4 + n = 10$ _6_

11 $n - 9 = 7$ _16_

12 $n + 6 = 14$ _8_

13 $18 - n = 9$ _9_

14 $17 = 9 + n$ _8_

Add or subtract.

15
$$53,487,403$$
$$- 24,059,357$$
_29,425,046_

16
$$40,972,195$$
$$+ 68,427,327$$
_109,399,522_

17
$$12,645$$
$$- 999$$
_11,646_

What is the right sign? Draw <, >, or =.

18 $5.21 ⊘ $5.19

19 $99.88 ⊘ $99.90

20 $0.44 ⊘ $4.04

Solve these problems.

21 Maria swam 16 laps on Monday and seven laps on Tuesday. How many laps did she swim all together? _____

22 How many more laps did Maria swim on Monday than she swam on Tuesday? _____

Add or subtract.

①
```
  7
  9
  8
+ 2
```
26

②
```
  5
  8
  4
+ 5
```
22

③
```
  9
  1
  6
+ 3
```
19

④
```
  8
  2
  3
+ 7
```
20

⑤
```
  $5.68
+   0.96
```
$884

⑥
```
  $6.89
+   3.08
```

⑦
```
  3581
+ 2789
```
9370

⑧
```
  6682
+  869
```
7551

⑨
```
  33,573
−  5,128
```

⑩
```
  42,804,167
+    646,809
```
43450978

⑪
```
  15,980
+  6,097
```
22077

⑫
```
  157,701
−  98,035
```

Solve these problems.

⑬ John wants to run eight laps around the track. If he runs five laps, has he run more than $\frac{1}{2}$ of them?

_____

⑭ If John has run six laps out of the eight he wants to run, what part of the total laps has he run?

_____

a. $\frac{1}{4}$　　b. $\frac{1}{2}$　　c. $\frac{3}{4}$

Name_____

Multiply. Compare the problems in each pair.

1 $2 \times 7 = n$ ___14___

    $7 \times 2 = n$ ___14___

4 $8 \times 0 = n$ ___0___

    $0 \times 8 = n$ ___0___

2 $1 \times 9 = n$ ___9___

    $9 \times 1 = n$ ___18___

5 $3 \times 6 = n$ _____

    $6 \times 3 = n$ ___18___

3 $5 \times 6 = n$ ___30___

    $6 \times 5 = n$ ___30___

6 $9 \times 4 = n$ ___36___

    $4 \times 9 = n$ ___36___

Multiply to solve for *n*.

7 $0 \times 4 = n$ ___0___

10 $4 \times 0 = n$ ___0___

13 $7 \times 1 = n$ ___7___

16 $1 \times 7 = n$ ___7___

19 $2 \times 8 = n$ ___16___

8 $5 \times 10 = n$ ___50___

11 $2 \times 7 = n$ ___14___ ___8___

14 $2 \times 9 = n$ _____

17 $8 \times 1 = n$ ___8___

20 $1 \times 10 = n$ ___10___

9 $5 \times 2 = n$ ___10___

12 $10 \times 3 = n$ ___30___

15 $5 \times 4 = n$ ___20___

18 $6 \times 0 = n$ ___0___

21 $10 \times 2 = n$ ___20___

Multiply.

22   6
  $\times 1$
  ___
  6

23   8
  $\times 2$
  ___
  16

24   6
  $\times 5$
  ___
  30

25   0
  $\times 9$
  ___
  0

26   9
  $\times 6$
  ___
  54

27   1
  $\times 6$
  ___
  6

28   2
  $\times 8$
  ___
  16

29   5
  $\times 6$
  ___
  30

30   9
  $\times 0$
  ___
  0

31   6
  $\times 3$
  ___
  18

32   5
  $\times 7$
  ___
  35

33   7
  $\times 2$
  ___
  14

34   7
  $\times 0$
  ___
  0

35   6
  $\times 6$
  ___
  36

36   5
  $\times 3$
  ___
  15

Name_____

Use the multiplication table to find these facts.

1 $7 \times 8 =$ _56_

2 $8 \times 8 =$ _84_

3 $8 \times 6 =$ _48_

4 $4 \times 8 =$ _32_

×	0	1	2	3	4	5	6	7	8	9	10
0	0	0	0	0	0	0	0	0	0	0	0
1	0	1	2	3	4	5	6	7	8	9	10
2	0	2	4	6	8	10	12	14	16	18	20
3	0	3	6	9	12	15	18	21	24	27	30
4	0	4	8	12	16	20	24	28	32	36	40
5	0	5	10	15	20	25	30	35	40	45	50
6	0	6	12	18	24	30	36	42	48	54	60
7	0	7	14	21	28	35	42	49	56	63	70
8	0	8	16	24	32	40	48	56	64	72	80
9	0	9	18	27	36	45	54	63	72	81	90
10	0	10	20	30	40	50	60	70	80	90	100

Use the multiplication table to compare columns marked 9 and 4.

5 What is 4×9? _____

6 What is 4×4? _____

7 What is 6×9? _____

8 What is 6×4? _____

9 What is 9×9? _____

10 What is 8×4? _____

Solve for n.

11 $8 \times 9 = n$ _72_

12 $7 \times 9 = n$ _63_

13 $6 \times 6 = n$ _36_

14 $7 \times 5 = n$ _35_

15 $9 \times 2 = n$ _18_

16 $2 \times 5 = n$ _10_

17 $8 \times 3 = n$ _24_

18 $5 \times 5 = n$ _25_

19 $3 \times 7 = n$ _21_

20 $10 \times 4 = n$ _40_

21 $9 \times 4 = n$ _36_

22 $5 \times 7 = n$ _35_

23 $8 \times 4 = n$ _32_

24 $8 \times 10 = n$ _80_

25 $9 \times 5 = n$ _45_

26 $6 \times 4 = n$ _24_

27 $7 \times 4 = n$ _28_

28 $10 \times 7 = n$ _70_

Name_____

Complete this multiplication table.

×	0	1	2	3	4	5	6	7	8	9	10
0	0	0	0	0	0	0	0	0	0	0	0
1	0	1	2	3	4	5	6	7	8	9	10
2	0	2	4	6	8	10	12	14	16	18	20
3	0	3	6	9	12	15	18	21	24	27	30
4	0	4	8	12	16	20	24	28	32	36	40
5	5	5	10	15	20	25	30	35	40	45	50
6	0	6	12	18	24	30	36	42	48	54	60
7	0	7	14	21	28	35	42	49	56	63	70
8	0	8	16	24	32	40	48	56	64	72	80
9	0	9	18	27	36	45	54	63	72	81	90
10	0	10	20	30	40	50	60	70	80	90	100

Solve for n.

1 $5 \times 0 = n$ _0_

2 $6 \times 6 = n$ _36_

3 $7 \times 5 = n$ _35_

4 $4 \times 3 = n$ _12_

5 $5 \times 9 = n$ _45_

6 $8 \times 4 = n$ _32_

7 $3 \times 7 = n$ _21_

8 $5 \times 8 = n$ _40_

9 $9 \times 3 = n$ _27_

10 $8 \times 6 = n$ _48_

11 $2 \times 8 = n$ _16_

12 $8 \times 3 = n$ _24_

Name_____

Look at the triangle and the three squares. See if you find anything interesting. Remember, to find the area of a square, multiply the length of a side by itself.

Answer these questions.

1 What is the area of the square with sides of 6 cm?

_____

2 What is the area of the square with sides of 8 cm?

_____

3 What is the area of the square with sides of 6 cm plus the area of the square with sides of 8 cm?

_____

4 What is the area of the square with sides of 10 cm? _____

5 What kind of triangle is this? _____

6 Do all of the squares have right angles? _____

To find the area of a square, multiply the length of a side by itself.

Complete the charts below.

	Length of Side	Area of Square
7	10 cm	
8	9 cm	
9	8 cm	
10	7 cm	
11	6 cm	

	Length of Side	Area of Square
12	5 cm	
13	4 cm	
14	3 cm	
15	2 cm	
16	1 cm	

LESSON
32
PRACTICE

Name_____

Solve for *n*.

1 $2 \times 3 = n$ _6_

2 $5 \times 6 = n$ _30_

3 $8 \times 5 = n$ _40_

4 $4 \times 5 = n$ _20_

5 $2 \times 8 = n$ _16_

6 $0 \times 7 = n$ _0_

7 $6 \times 8 = n$ _48_

8 $n = 3 \times 8$ _24_

9 $5 \times 1 = n$ _5_

10 $7 \times 1 = n$ _7_

11 $n = 9 \times 2$ _18_

12 $3 \times 7 = n$ _21_

13 $0 \times 10 = n$ _0_

14 $n = 7 \times 6$ _42_

15 $8 \times 8 = n$ _64_

16 $5 \times 7 = n$ _35_

17 $n = 6 \times 9$ _54_

18 $n = 16 \times 3$ _48_

19 $n = 8 \times 4$ _32_

20 $n = 4 \times 4$ _16_

21 $n = 5 \times 5$ _25_

22 $n = 3 \times 5$ _15_

23 $n = 7 \times 8$ _56_

24 $9 \times 6 = n$ _54_

25 $8 \times 7 = n$ _56_

26 $6 \times 7 = n$ _42_

27 $4 \times 8 = n$ _32_

28 $n = 5 \times 9$ _45_

29 $n = 3 \times 9$ _27_

30 $6 \times 2 = n$ _12_

Multiply.

31 $\begin{array}{r} 10 \\ \times\ 8 \\ \hline 80 \end{array}$
32 $\begin{array}{r} 9 \\ \times\ 9 \\ \hline 81 \end{array}$
33 $\begin{array}{r} 7 \\ \times\ 7 \\ \hline 49 \end{array}$
34 $\begin{array}{r} 8 \\ \times\ 1 \\ \hline 8 \end{array}$
35 $\begin{array}{r} 9 \\ \times\ 6 \\ \hline 54 \end{array}$
36 $\begin{array}{r} 7 \\ \times\ 9 \\ \hline 63 \end{array}$

37 $\begin{array}{r} 7 \\ \times\ 4 \\ \hline 28 \end{array}$
38 $\begin{array}{r} 4 \\ \times\ 5 \\ \hline 20 \end{array}$
39 $\begin{array}{r} 4 \\ \times\ 9 \\ \hline 36 \end{array}$
40 $\begin{array}{r} 9 \\ \times\ 3 \\ \hline 27 \end{array}$
41 $\begin{array}{r} 9 \\ \times\ 2 \\ \hline 18 \end{array}$
42 $\begin{array}{r} 5 \\ \times\ 2 \\ \hline 10 \end{array}$

43 $\begin{array}{r} 10 \\ \times\ 0 \\ \hline 0 \end{array}$
44 $\begin{array}{r} 2 \\ \times\ 5 \\ \hline \end{array}$
45 $\begin{array}{r} 9 \\ \times\ 7 \\ \hline 63 \end{array}$
46 $\begin{array}{r} 9 \\ \times\ 8 \\ \hline \end{array}$
47 $\begin{array}{r} 5 \\ \times\ 8 \\ \hline \end{array}$
48 $\begin{array}{r} 3 \\ \times\ 3 \\ \hline 9 \end{array}$

Name_____

Are You Shiny or Rusty?
Very shiny   39 or more right
Shiny   34–38 right
A bit rusty   29–33 right
Rusty   Fewer than 29 right

Multiply.

1 0 _____ $= 0 \times 8$

2 $5 \times 5 = \underline{25}$

3 $\underline{10} = 5 \times 2$

4 $\underline{15} = 5 \times 3$

5 $\underline{27} = 3 \times 9$

6 $\underline{24} = 6 \times 4$

7 $\underline{4} = 1 \times 4$

8 $4 \times 8 = \underline{32}$

9 $\underline{8} = 8 \times 1$

10 $\underline{21} = 7 \times 3$

11 $\underline{49} = 7 \times 7$

12 $2 \times 7 = \underline{14}$

13 $6 \times 6 = \underline{36}$

14 $5 \times 8 = \underline{40}$

15 $8 \times 9 = \underline{72}$

16 $8 \times 6 = \underline{48}$

17 $2 \times 6 = \underline{12}$

18 $4 \times 7 = \underline{28}$

19 $\underline{12} = 4 \times 3$

20 $\underline{30} = 6 \times 5$

21 $\underline{36} = 4 \times 9$

22 $6 \times 7 = \underline{42}$

23 $\underline{24} = 8 \times 3$

24 $\underline{0} = 3 \times 0$

25 $\underline{32} = 8 \times 4$

26 $10 \times 3 = \underline{30}$

27 $\underline{63} = 9 \times 7$

28 $\underline{60} = 6 \times 10$

29 $\underline{42} = 7 \times 6$

30 $2 \times 9 = \underline{18}$

31 $\underline{27} = 3 \times 9$

32 $5 \times 3 = \underline{15}$

Multiply.

33
$\begin{array}{r} 5 \\ \times\ 4 \\ \hline 20 \end{array}$

34
$\begin{array}{r} 3 \\ \times\ 2 \\ \hline 6 \end{array}$

35
$\begin{array}{r} 7 \\ \times\ 0 \\ \hline 0 \end{array}$

36
$\begin{array}{r} 8 \\ \times\ 8 \\ \hline 64 \end{array}$

37
$\begin{array}{r} 8 \\ \times\ 6 \\ \hline 48 \end{array}$

38
$\begin{array}{r} 4 \\ \times\ 9 \\ \hline 36 \end{array}$

39
$\begin{array}{r} 7 \\ \times\ 1 \\ \hline 7 \end{array}$

40
$\begin{array}{r} 9 \\ \times\ 6 \\ \hline 54 \end{array}$

41
$\begin{array}{r} 4 \\ \times\ 4 \\ \hline 16 \end{array}$

42
$\begin{array}{r} 6 \\ \times\ 3 \\ \hline 18 \end{array}$

43
$\begin{array}{r} 7 \\ \times\ 6 \\ \hline 42 \end{array}$

44
$\begin{array}{r} 5 \\ \times\ 3 \\ \hline 15 \end{array}$

Name_____

Complete the function charts.

1

×3	
In	**Out**
0	0
2	6
4	12
6	18
8	24

2

×4	
In	**Out**
1	4
3	12
5	20
7	28
9	36

3

×5	
In	**Out**
4	20
5	25
6	30
7	35
8	40

Save-More is having a half-price sale on pens. The manager asks you to make a half-price chart. This has been started for you.

Complete the chart. Use play money for help if you need it.

4

Price (in cents)	60	70	80	90	100
Half price (in cents)	30	35	40	45	50

Use the chart above to solve these problems.

5 How much will you pay for a pen that normally costs $1.00? _____

6 How much will you pay for two pens that are regularly priced at 70¢ each? _____

7 How much will you save when you buy a pen at half price that was regularly priced at 90¢? _____

Name_____

High school basketball rules call for the following times.

Regulation Time

The four quarters are each eight minutes long.
The break between the first and second quarters and between the third and fourth quarters is one minute.
The break between the second and third quarters is ten minutes.
The clock can be stopped for various reasons, which adds to the length of a game.

Overtime

If a game is tied, three minutes of overtime are allowed. There is a one-minute break between overtime periods if needed.

Answer these questions.

How long will a basketball game last if time

1 is not stopped and there is no overtime?   _____

2 is stopped for ten minutes and there is one overtime?   _____

3 is stopped for 25 minutes but there is no overtime?

_____

4 is stopped for 30 minutes and there are two overtimes?

_____

5 is stopped for $10\frac{1}{2}$ minutes and there are two overtimes?

_____

6 is stopped for $22\frac{1}{2}$ minutes and there are three overtimes?

_____

Name_____

For each problem the measure in one of the statements makes more sense than the other. Choose the one that makes more sense. If you think both make sense, explain why.

1 I rode my bike $2\frac{1}{2}$ miles or **4400 yards**. _____

2 Mr. Harvey's car weighs about **2000 pounds** or **1 ton**. _____

3 Mrs. Chung is going to buy a **3-pound** or **48-ounce** bag of apples. _____

4 My finger is about **3 inches** or $\frac{1}{4}$ **foot** long. _____

5 My cat Ginger weighs about **15 pounds** or **240 ounces**. _____

6 This package of cream cheese contains **8 ounces** or $\frac{1}{2}$ **pound**. _____

7 I am going to buy **128 ounces** or **1 gallon** of ice cream. _____

8 This piece of paper is about **1 foot** or **12 inches** long. _____

9 I want to buy **16 ounces** or **1 pound** of lunch meat. _____

10 The bottle contains **12 ounces** or $1\frac{1}{2}$ **cups** of hand lotion. _____

11 My brother is **48 inches** or $1\frac{1}{3}$ **yards** tall. _____

12 Jonathan walks about $1\frac{1}{2}$ **miles** or **7920 feet** to school every day. _____

13 A box of crackers contains **8 ounces** or $\frac{1}{2}$ **pound**. _____

14 My aunt weighs **150 pounds** or $\frac{1}{8}$ **ton**. _____

15 I drink **64 ounces** or **8 cups** of water each day. _____

16 I am going to fill my speedboat with **20 gallons** or **80 quarts** of gasoline. _____

17 My foot is about $\frac{3}{4}$ **foot** or **9 inches** long. _____

Name_____

Units of Length	Units of Weight	Units of Volume	United States Currency	Number in Basic Unit
millimeter	milligram	milliliter	mill	1000
centimeter	centigram	centiliter	cent	100
decimeter	decigram	deciliter	dime	10
meter*	gram	liter*	dollar*	1
dekameter	dekagram	dekaliter	10 dollars	0.1
hectometer	hectogram	hectoliter	100 dollars	0.01
kilometer	kilogram*	kiloliter	1000 dollars	0.001

*Basic units

Use the chart to answer these questions.

❶ How many milligrams are in 1 gram? _____

❷ How many deciliters are in 1 liter? _____

❸ How many dimes are in $10? _____

❹ How many grams are in 1 hectogram? _____

❺ How many hectometers are in 1 kilometer? _____

❻ How many cents are in $100? _____

❼ How many centiliters are in 1 liter? _____

❽ How many mills are in 1 dime? _____

❾ How many dimes are in $100? _____

❿ Find three items that are measured in kilometers. _____

⓫ Find three items that are measured in milligrams. _____

Choose the measure that makes more sense. If you think both make sense, explain why.

1 I bought **1 kilogram** or **1000 grams** of grapes.   _____

2 This bag of pretzels weighs **750 grams** or **75,000 milligrams.**   _____

3 I rode my bike **2.4 kilometers** or **2400 meters.**   _____

4 My arm is about **60 centimeters** or **0.6 meters** long.   _____

5 My dog Sam weighs about **16 kilograms** or **16,000 grams.**   _____

6 This bottle of juice holds about **2 liters** or **0.02 kiloliters.**   _____

7 I am going to buy a turkey that weighs **8 kilograms** or **8000 grams.**   _____

8 My library card is about **6 centimeters** or **0.06 meters** long.   _____

9 The bottle holds **1 liter** or **1000 milliliters** of water.   _____

10 My baby sister is **50 centimeters** or $\frac{1}{2}$ **meter tall.**   _____

11 My father drives about **30 kilometers** or **3000 meters** to work every day.   _____

12 A bag of sugar weighs about **2.2 kilograms** or **2200 grams.**   _____

13 Each morning I drink a glass that holds $\frac{1}{4}$ **liter** or **250 milliliters** of grapefruit juice.   _____

14 My bed is about **2 meters** or **2000 centimeters** wide.   _____

15 Mr. Bruce is going to buy about $\frac{1}{2}$ **kilogram** or **500 grams** of peanuts.   _____

16 This quarter weighs about **8 grams** or **8000 milligrams.**   _____

Daniel is thinking of a rectangle. He says, "It is at least 3 centimeters long but no more than 4 centimeters long. It is at least 1 centimeter wide, but no more than 2 centimeters wide."

Which of these rectangles can be the one Daniel is thinking of? Write yes or no for each one. Use a centimeter ruler to measure.

1

2

3

_____   _____   _____

Complete this chart about children's play areas. Draw diagrams to help you.

Play area	Length (meters)		Width (meters)		Area (square meters)	
	At least	No more than	At least	No more than	At least	No more than
4 Lon's	8	9	7	8	56	
5 Carrie's	7	8	5	6		
6 William's	6	7	5	6		
7 Mary's	5	6	8	9		
8 Jesse's	8	9	5	7		

Are You Shiny or Rusty?

Very shiny   37 or more right
Shiny   32–36 right
A bit rusty   27–31 right
Rusty   Fewer than 27 right

Solve for *n*.

1 $5 \times 10 = n$ ___ 50

2 $9 \times 7 = n$ ___ 63

3 $2 \times 4 = n$ ___ 8

4 $6 \times 3 = n$ ___ 18

5 $5 \times 9 = n$ ___ 45

6 $7 \times 2 = n$ ___ 14

7 $9 \times 0 = n$ ___ 0

8 $7 \times 7 = n$ ___ 49

9 $6 \times 7 = n$ ___ 42

10 $4 \times 5 = n$ ___ 20

11 $2 \times 9 = n$ ___ 18

12 $7 \times 3 = n$ ___ 21

13 $6 \times 8 = n$ ___ 48

14 $5 \times 6 = n$ ___ 30

15 $8 \times 7 = n$ ___ 56

16 $2 \times 6 = n$ ___ 12

17 $9 \times 10 = n$ ___ 90

18 $2 \times 5 = n$ ___ 10

19 $5 \times 8 = n$ ___ 40

20 $6 \times 6 = n$ ___ 36

21 $9 \times 1 = n$ ___ 9

22 $4 \times 6 = n$ ___ 24

23 $7 \times 9 = n$ ___ 63

24 $2 \times 3 = n$ ___ 6

Multiply.

25 8
       × 0
        0

26 5
       × 5
       25

27 2
       × 8
       18

28 10
       × 4
        40

29 1
       × 5
        5

30 7
       × 2

31 7
       × 6
       42

32 10
       × 3
        30

33 5
       × 8
       40

34 6
       × 9
       54

35 9
       × 9
       81

36 3
       × 8
       24

37 3
       × 6
       18

38 1
       × 6
        6

39 2
       × 2
        4

40 8
       × 3
       24

41 5
       × 7
       35

42 2
       × 9
       18

Solve these problems.

1 Bill earns $5 each time he cleans his grandmother's house. How many times will he have to clean his grandmother's house to earn the $25 he needs for a new basketball? _____

2 Andrea rides her mountain bike four times each week. She rode the same distance every day last week, and she rode a total of 12 miles. How many miles did she ride each day? _____

3 In the school cafeteria the cooks use four cans of tomatoes to make soup for a day's lunch. They have 24 cans of tomatoes. How many days can they make this soup for lunch with the cans of tomatoes they have? _____

4 There are four quarters in a football game. The total playing time of a football game is 32 minutes. How long is each quarter? _____

Solve for *n*.

5 $8 \times n = 48$ _____

6 $7 \times n = 56$ _____

7 $6 \times n = 42$ _____

8 $4 \times n = 28$ _____

9 $5 \times n = 50$ _____

10 $4 \times n = 12$ _____

11 $7 \times n = 42$ _____

12 $6 \times n = 54$ _____

13 $8 \times n = 48$ _____

14 $54 = n \times 9$ _____

15 $n \times 4 = 24$ _____

16 $7 \times n = 35$ _____

17 $7 \times n = 63$ _____

18 $8 \times n = 32$ _____

19 $9 \times n = 36$ _____

20 $64 = 8 \times n$ _____

21 $n \times 6 = 18$ _____

22 $9 \times n = 45$ _____

23 $5 \times n = 25$ _____

24 $10 \times n = 80$ _____

25 $n \times 3 = 9$ _____

26 $27 = 9 \times n$ _____

27 $5 \times n = 35$ _____

28 $6 \times n = 54$ _____

29 $1 \times n = 10$ _____

30 $n \times 8 = 72$ _____

31 $n \times 5 = 45$ _____

Name_____

Divide.

1 20 ÷ 4 = _____ **2** 27 ÷ 3 = _____ **3** 28 ÷ 4 = _____

4 16 ÷ 8 = _____ **5** 36 ÷ 6 = _____ **6** 72 ÷ 9 = _____

7 9 ÷ 1 = _____ **8** 42 ÷ 7 = _____ **9** 40 ÷ 4 = _____

10 24 ÷ 6 = _____ **11** 27 ÷ 9 = _____ **12** 30 ÷ 3 = _____

13 30 ÷ 10 = _____ **14** 56 ÷ 8 = _____ **15** 25 ÷ 5 = _____

Divide.

16 1)‾10‾ **17** 4)‾28‾ **18** 7)‾21‾ **19** 6)‾30‾

20 7)‾35‾ **21** 2)‾18‾ **22** 8)‾24‾ **23** 4)‾40‾

24 3)‾21‾ **25** 6)‾36‾ **26** 9)‾18‾ **27** 6)‾42‾

Solve these problems.

28 Beth earns $6 for each hour of work. She made $48 today. How many hours did she work today? _____

29 When Beth works overtime, she only has to work 4 hours to make $36. How much does she earn each hour working overtime? _____

30 On a game show each correct answer is worth ten points. Team A scores 90 points and Team B scores 70 points. How many correct answers did each team have? _____

Name_____

Solve for *n*. Watch the signs.

1 $8 + 5 = n$ _____   **2** $10 = 3 + n$ _____   **3** $10 = 15 - n$ _____

4 $14 - 7 = n$ _____   **5** $14 = 6 + n$ _____   **6** $16 - n = 9$ _____

7 $8 - 8 = n$ _____   **8** $n = 11 - 7$ _____   **9** $10 - 0 = n$ _____

10 $9 + 9 = n$ _____   **11** $11 = n + 3$ _____   **12** $9 + n = 17$ _____

Add or subtract. Use shortcuts when you can.

13 $\begin{array}{r} 45 \\ + 67 \\ \hline \end{array}$	**14** $\begin{array}{r} 1500 \\ - 500 \\ \hline \end{array}$	**15** $\begin{array}{r} 7215 \\ - 3215 \\ \hline \end{array}$	**16** $\begin{array}{r} 450 \\ + 250 \\ \hline \end{array}$	**17** $\begin{array}{r} 450 \\ - 260 \\ \hline \end{array}$
18 $\begin{array}{r} 92 \\ - 38 \\ \hline \end{array}$	**19** $\begin{array}{r} 77 \\ + 29 \\ \hline \end{array}$	**20** $\begin{array}{r} 2710 \\ - 2699 \\ \hline \end{array}$	**21** $\begin{array}{r} 600 \\ - 550 \\ \hline \end{array}$	**22** $\begin{array}{r} 850 \\ + 59 \\ \hline \end{array}$
23 $\begin{array}{r} 581 \\ - 244 \\ \hline \end{array}$	**24** $\begin{array}{r} 297 \\ + 603 \\ \hline \end{array}$	**25** $\begin{array}{r} 6424 \\ - 28 \\ \hline \end{array}$	**26** $\begin{array}{r} 700 \\ - 699 \\ \hline \end{array}$	**27** $\begin{array}{r} 554 \\ + 265 \\ \hline \end{array}$

Solve for *n*. Watch the signs.

28 $9 \times 3 = n$ _____   **29** $28 \div 7 = n$ _____   **30** $12 \div n = 3$ _____

31 $56 \div 8 = n$ _____   **32** $15 \div 3 = n$ _____   **33** $49 = n \times 7$ _____

34 $8 \times 8 = n$ _____   **35** $10 \times 8 = n$ _____   **36** $32 = 4 \times n$ _____

37 $18 \div 2 = n$ _____   **38** $8 \times n = 40$ _____   **39** $10 \times n = 100$ _____

Four boys decided to collect aluminum cans, plastic, and paper from the neighborhood. When they collected these recyclable items, they took them to the recycling center. Sometimes they found money along the way. At the end of each week they divided all their money equally.

Use play money to act out these problems and answer the questions.

1 The first week they got $28 for their items at the recycling center. They also found $4 in cash.

a. How much money did they get all together? _____

b. How much money should each boy get? _____

2 The second week they got $30 at the recycling center. They also found $6 in cash.

a. How much money did they get all together? _____

b. How much money should each boy get? _____

3 The third week they got $25 at the recycling center. They also found $5 in cash.

a. How much money did they get all together? _____

b. If they only have one-dollar bills, how many one-dollar bills should each boy get? _____

c. How many one-dollar bills are left over? _____

Divide. Watch for remainders.

4 $5\overline{)30}$ **5** $7\overline{)20}$ **6** $4\overline{)21}$ **7** $8\overline{)56}$ **8** $6\overline{)28}$

Divide. Watch for remainders.

1 2$\overline{)7}$　　　　**2** 9$\overline{)19}$　　　　**3** 3$\overline{)10}$　　　　**4** 7$\overline{)10}$

5 2$\overline{)8}$　　　　**6** 3$\overline{)22}$　　　　**7** 3$\overline{)11}$　　　　**8** 9$\overline{)52}$

9 2$\overline{)9}$　　　　**10** 4$\overline{)14}$　　　　**11** 3$\overline{)12}$　　　　**12** 9$\overline{)53}$

13 3$\overline{)14}$　　　　**14** 10$\overline{)37}$　　　　**15** 2$\overline{)9}$　　　　**16** 6$\overline{)50}$

17 3$\overline{)15}$　　　　**18** 9$\overline{)13}$　　　　**19** 4$\overline{)38}$　　　　**20** 4$\overline{)30}$

21 2$\overline{)19}$　　　　**22** 6$\overline{)7}$　　　　**23** 5$\overline{)43}$　　　　**24** 8$\overline{)65}$

25 5$\overline{)31}$　　　　**26** 7$\overline{)34}$　　　　**27** 9$\overline{)24}$　　　　**28** 6$\overline{)25}$

Solve these problems.

29 Maria needs to buy 29 sodas for a party. The sodas come six to a pack. Each six-pack costs $2.00.

a. How many six-packs must Maria buy?　　　_____

b. If Maria buys five six-packs, how many sodas will she have?　　　_____

c. How much will it cost for Maria to buy enough sodas?　　　_____

You can use a table to find multiples and common multiples.

Complete these tables and answer the question.

❶

	×0	×1	×2	×3	×4	×5	×6	×7	×8	×9	×10
Multiples of 3		3				15					

❷

	×0	×1	×2	×3	×4	×5	×6	×7	×8	×9	×10
Multiples of 4			8					28			

❸ What are the common multiples of 3 and 4? _____

Find the first three common multiples of each pair of numbers.

❹ 4 and 10 _____, _____, _____   **❺** 3 and 5 _____, _____, _____

❻ 8 and 10 _____, _____, _____   **❼** 2 and 7 _____, _____, _____

❽ 6 and 8 _____, _____, _____   **❾** 5 and 8 _____, _____, _____

❿ 4 and 12 _____, _____, _____   **⓫** 3 and 9 _____, _____, _____

⓬ 7 and 14 _____, _____, _____   **⓭** 7 and 9 _____, _____, _____

⓮ 5 and 6 _____, _____, _____   **⓯** 3 and 12 _____, _____, _____

Answer these questions.

⓰ In which problems is there a whole number greater than 1 that divides evenly into both numbers?

_____

⓱ If there is a common factor for the pair of numbers, how is the first multiple different?

_____

Solve for *n*. Watch the parentheses. Watch the signs.

1 $32 \div (8 \div 2) = n$ _____
2 $16 - (6 - 5) = n$ _____
3 $(18 - 5) + 5 = n$ _____

4 $(32 \div 8) \div 2 = n$ _____
5 $(16 - 6) - 5 = n$ _____
6 $18 - (5 + 5) = n$ _____

7 $28 - (4 \div 4) = n$ _____
8 $(3 \times 2) \times 3 = n$ _____
9 $(48 \div 8) \div 2 = n$ _____

10 $(28 - 4) \div 4 = n$ _____
11 $3 \times (2 \times 3) = n$ _____
12 $48 \div (8 \div 2) = n$ _____

13 $4 \times (3 + 6) = n$ _____
14 $(36 \div 6) \div 3 = n$ _____
15 $(4 \times 3) \times 2 = n$ _____

16 $(4 \times 5) + 6 = n$ _____
17 $36 \div (6 \div 3) = n$ _____
18 $4 \times (3 \times 2) = n$ _____

19 $16 + (6 + 5) = n$ _____
20 $(24 - 12) - 8 = n$ _____
21 $24 - (12 - 8) = n$ _____

22 $(16 + 6) + 5 = n$ _____
23 $6 \times (5 - 5) = n$ _____
24 $(6 \times 5) - 5 = n$ _____

For each problem below show how many different answers you can get by putting parentheses in different places.

25 $18 - 10 + 2 = n$ _____
26 $3 \times 3 + 4 = n$ _____
27 $5 \times 6 \div 3 = n$ _____

28 $16 + 4 \times 2 = n$ _____
29 $16 \div 4 \times 4 = n$ _____
30 $16 - 3 \times 2 = n$ _____

31 $3 \times 3 \times 4 = n$ _____
32 $12 - 6 \div 3 = n$ _____
33 $12 + 2 + 3 = n$ _____

34 $6 + 8 + 6 = n$ _____
35 $18 - 6 + 6 = n$ _____
36 $14 \times 2 + 1 = n$ _____

37 $24 \div 3 \div 1 = n$ _____
38 $24 \div 6 \times 2 = n$ _____
39 $24 \div 6 \div 2 = n$ _____

Use a calculator to solve each of the following in three different ways.

40 $3 \times 4 \times 5 \times 6 = n$ _____
41 $3 + 4 + 5 + 6 = n$ _____

42 $3 \times 4 + 5 \times 6 = n$ _____
43 $3 + 4 \times 5 + 6 = n$ _____

44 $3 \times 4 \times 5 + 6 = n$ _____
45 $3 + 4 + 5 \times 6 = n$ _____

Solve these problems.

1 Ray had $8.00 and then spent some of it. He now has $5.75. How much money did he spend?

_____

2 Jake has collected 736 aluminum cans for recycling. The recycling center pays 1¢ per can. How much money will Jake get?

_____

3 Gillian is building a kite. She needs two pieces of balsa that are each 31 centimeters long and one piece that is 37 centimeters long. How much balsa does she need all together?

_____

4 Miss Hawk's garden is 8 meters long and 6 meters wide. What is its area?

_____

5 Pedro has invited 17 people to a party. He wants to serve each of them one can of cola. How many cartons of cola should he buy if there are six cans of cola in each carton?

_____

6 Robert had $281.60 in the bank. He withdrew $110.50 to buy a bicycle. How much does he have left in the bank?

_____

7 If 40 baseball cards are to be divided equally among five children, how many cards should each child get?

_____

8 The Abbot family and the Graham family visit a Civil War battlefield. Tickets cost $5 each. The Abbots buy six tickets and the Grahams buy four tickets. How much do the two families spend all together?

_____

9 The Abbots go again on a weekday when the tickets are only $3 each for the six of them. They also pay $2 to park. How much do the Abbots spend in all on this day?

_____

Name_____

Multiply.

1 $9 \times 5 =$ _____ 46

2 $8 \times 8 =$ _____ 64

3 $7 \times 6 =$ _____ 42

4 $9 \times 4 =$ _____ 36

5 $4 \times 6 =$ _____ 24

6 $5 \times 7 =$ _____ 35

7 $7 \times 8 =$ _____ 56

8 $8 \times 5 =$ _____ 40

Divide. Don't forget remainders.

9 $9\overline{)19}$

10 $4\overline{)38}$

11 $7\overline{)60}$

12 $3\overline{)25}$

13 $10 \div 5 =$ _____ 2

14 $54 \div 9 =$ _____

15 $28 \div 7 =$ _____

16 $24 \div 3 =$ _____ 8

17 $3\overline{)23}$

18 $9\overline{)82}$

19 $7\overline{)50}$

20 $6\overline{)42}$

Solve. Watch the signs.

21 $\begin{array}{r} 8 \\ + 5 \\ \hline \end{array}$

22 $\begin{array}{r} 12 \\ - 8 \\ \hline \end{array}$

23 $\begin{array}{r} 7 \\ + 3 \\ \hline \end{array}$

24 $\begin{array}{r} 248 \\ - 163 \\ \hline \end{array}$

25 $\begin{array}{r} 408 \\ + 682 \\ \hline \end{array}$

Solve for *n*. Watch the signs.

26 $n - 6 = 12$ _____ 6

27 $n + 8 = 14$ _____ 6

28 $5 = 20 \div n$ _____ 4

29 $10 - n = 4$ _____ 6

30 $7 + n = 15$ _____ 8

31 $36 \div n = 6$ _____ 6

Solve these problems.

32 Bill has 45 stickers to give to six friends.

    a. How many stickers will each friend get?

    _____

    b. How many stickers will be left over?

    _____

LESSON
50 PRACTICE

Name_____

Solve for *n*. Watch the parentheses. Watch the signs.

1 $4 \times (4 + 5) = n$ _____

2 $16 - (9 - 7) = n$ _____

3 $n = (2 \times 5) + (4 \times 4)$ _____

4 $n = (6 + 8) - 5$ _____

5 $6 + (3 \times 2) = n$ _____

6 $6 \times (7 - 3) = n$ _____

Solve for *n*. Watch the signs.

7 $n = 10 \times 5$ _____

8 $5 \times n = 25$ _____

9 $n \times 9 = 63$ _____

10 $n - 10 = 40$ _____

11 $25 - n = 18$ _____

12 $n = 65 - 46$ _____

13 $8 + 5 = n$ _____

14 $6 + n = 13$ _____

15 $n - 18 = 65$ _____

16 $n = 64 \div 8$ _____

17 $n \div 4 = 7$ _____

18 $81 \div n = 9$ _____

Divide. Remember the remainders.

19 $7\overline{)42}$

20 $5\overline{)45}$

21 $6\overline{)30}$

22 $8\overline{)32}$

23 $3\overline{)18}$

24 $7\overline{)45}$

25 $9\overline{)50}$

26 $3\overline{)25}$

27 $4\overline{)26}$

28 $7\overline{)23}$

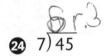

Solve these problems.

Constance wants to buy 45 balloons. Balloons come in bags of ten.

29 How many bags should she buy? _____

30 How many extra balloons will she have? _____

Square City

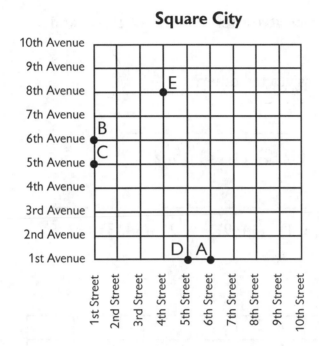

Suppose the people of Square City agree to always give the street name first and the avenue name second.

1 Where is the corner of 6th and 1st? _____

2 Where is the corner of 1st and 6th? _____

3 How many blocks would you have to walk to get from 6th and 1st to 1st and 6th? (You must not cut across blocks.) _____

4 Is there more than one way to get from 6th and 1st to 1st and 6th by walking only ten blocks? _____

Give the location of these points on the map of Square City. Remember to give the street name first and the avenue name second.

5 C _____

6 D _____

7 E _____

Name_____

Use the code graph to translate ordered pairs to letters and answer the riddle.

What did one math book say to the other?

____ , ____ ____   ____ ____ ____

(1, 1)   (12, 10) (4, 2)   (4, 10) (12, 8) (8, 9)

____ ____ ____ ____ ____ ____ ____ ____ .

(10, 2) (5, 8) (12, 8) (8, 1) (14, 9) (4, 2) (14, 3) (12, 5)

Find a function rule for each set of arrow operations.

1 _____

10 —(?)→ 6

12 —(?)→ 8

14 —(?)→ 10

4 —(?)→ 0

2 _____

6 —(?)→ 30

2 —(?)→ 10

4 —(?)→ 20

5 —(?)→ 25

3 _____

20 —(?)→ 10

16 —(?)→ 8

12 —(?)→ 6

10 —(?)→ 5

4 _____

11 —(?)→ 17

8 —(?)→ 14

6 —(?)→ 12

24 —(?)→ 30

5 _____

0 —(?)→ 0

2 —(?)→ 4

6 —(?)→ 12

8 —(?)→ 16

6 _____

6 —(?)→ 6

4 —(?)→ 4

0 —(?)→ 0

50 —(?)→ 50

In each case, tell what y is.

7 14 —(+6)→ y   y = _____

8 27 —(−6)→ y   y = _____

9 10 —(÷2)→ y   y = _____

10 11 —(×6)→ y   y = _____

11 16 —(÷4)→ y   y = _____

12 16 —(÷2)→ y   y = _____

13 9 —(+8)→ y   y = _____

14 7 —(×5)→ y   y = _____

Name_____

Find the value of x. Use inverse arrow operations if they help you.

1 x ———(+2)——▶ 9   x = _____

2 x ———(−12)——▶ 28   x = _____

3 x ———(−3)——▶ 12   x = _____

4 x ———(+9)——▶ 19   x = _____

5 x ———(+1)——▶ 20   x = _____

6 x ———(+3)——▶ 27   x = _____

7 x ———(+10)——▶ 90   x = _____

8 x ———(÷5)——▶ 25   x = _____

9 x ———(+10)——▶ 45   x = _____

10 x ———(÷7)——▶ 9   x = _____

11 x ———(−9)——▶ 41   x = _____

12 x ———(×9)——▶ 72   x = _____

13 x ———(÷10)——▶ 8   x = _____

14 x ———(+20)——▶ 60   x = _____

15 x ———(+100)——▶ 200   x = _____

16 x ———(−8)——▶ 22   x = _____

17 x ———(+50)——▶ 150   x = _____

18 150 ———(−50)——▶ x   x = _____

19 x ———(÷5)——▶ 17   x = _____

20 17 ———(×5)——▶ x   x = _____

21 x ———(×8)——▶ 64   x = _____

22 64 ———(÷8)——▶ x   x = _____

23 x ———(−0)——▶ 21   x = _____

24 21 ———(+0)——▶ x   x = _____

25 x ———(+30)——▶ 75   x = _____

26 75 ———(−30)——▶ x   x = _____

27 x ———(÷6)——▶ 6   x = _____

28 6 ———(×6)——▶ x   x = _____

29 x ———(+25)——▶ 75   x = _____

30 75 ———(−25)——▶ x   x = _____

Name_____

Copy each list of ordered pairs but replace the *x* or *y* with the correct number.

❶ x —(−4)→ y (10, 6), (7, *y*), (*x*, 12), (10, *y*), (*x*, 0)   _____

❷ x —(×3)→ y (3, *y*), (*x*, 12), (0, *y*), (*x*, 3), (*x*, 15)   _____

❸ x —(+1)→ y (0, *y*), (*x*, 2), (2, *y*), (*x*, 4), (20, *y*)   _____

Use function rules to answer the questions. Find the value of *x* or *y* in each ordered pair. Then use the code to find what letter each number represents.

X	O	L	M	R	S	T	H	I	E	W	Y	N
1	2	3	4	5	6	7	8	9	10	11	12	13

B	U	D	G	J	V	A	K	Z	C	P	Q	F
14	15	16	17	18	19	20	21	22	23	24	25	26

❹ What is the largest member of the cat family?

Use this function rule: x —(+5)→ y

___ ___ ___ ___ ___ ___ ___ ___

(1, *y*) (4, *y*) (9, *y*) (5, *y*) (0, *y*) (4, *y*) (15, *y*) (8, *y*)

___ ___ ___ ___ ___

(2, *y*) (4, *y*) (12, *y*) (5, *y*) (0, *y*)

Name_____

Complete these charts.

1 x ——(÷6)——> y

x	y
36	
	5
24	
18	
	1

2 x ——(×4)——> y

x	y
	20
	0
2	
8	
	28

3 x ——(−6)——> y

x	y
20	
	24
40	
	44
60	

Find the function rules before you complete these charts.

_____

4 x ——(?)——> y

x	y
5	
10	20
	25
50	
100	110

_____

5 x ——(?)——> y

x	y
12	
	3
10	2
	1
8	0

_____

6 x ——(?)——> y

x	y
2	
5	5
0	0
	100
50	

In each problem two of the answers are clearly wrong and one is correct. Choose the correct answer.

❶ 309
  + 617
  a. 2016
  b. 326
  c. 926

❷ 597
  − 498
  a. 1095
  b. 199
  c. 99

❸ 402
  − 142
  a. 360
  b. 544
  c. 260

❹ 745
  − 337
  a. 408
  b. 1008
  c. 112

❺ 643
  − 278
  a. 365
  b. 165
  c. 835

❻ 850
  + 759
  a. 91
  b. 1609
  c. 1509

❼ 3295
  − 2167
  a. 128
  b. 1128
  c. 5128

❽ 1647
  + 9353
  a. 20,000
  b. 8000
  c. 11,000

❾ 6439
  − 5161
  a. 1278
  b. 1338
  c. 11,600

❿ 525
  + 985
  a. 460
  b. 1510
  c. 4510

⓫ 243
  − 77
  a. 166
  b. 316
  c. 66

⓬ 685
  + 85
  a. 600
  b. 770
  c. 785

⓭ 5467
  + 3261
  a. 8728
  b. 828
  c. 1728

⓮ 433
  + 267
  a. 700
  b. 890
  c. 290

⓯ 433
  − 253
  a. 180
  b. 220
  c. 686

⓰ 5603
  − 5346
  a. 8257
  b. 1257
  c. 257

⓱ 526
  + 397
  a. 1523
  b. 223
  c. 923

⓲ 805
  + 805
  a. 805
  b. 0
  c. 1610

⓳ 260
  + 437
  a. 297
  b. 697
  c. 237

⓴ 3103
  − 2568
  a. 535
  b. 5035
  c. 135

㉑ 4130
  − 255
  a. 3975
  b. 3875
  c. 4125

㉒ 466
  + 466
  a. 932
  b. 822
  c. 0

㉓ 2206
  − 1150
  a. 1156
  b. 1056
  c. 3356

㉔ 5485
  + 3741
  a. 1744
  b. 8125
  c. 9226

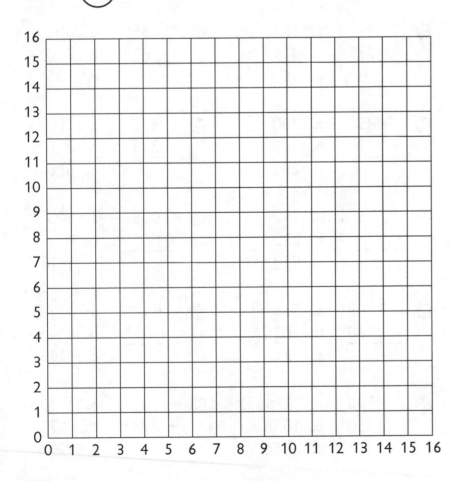

Name_____

Replace *x* or *y* with the correct number. (One has been done for you.) Then graph each set of ordered pairs.

❶ *x* ⟶ (+6) ⟶ *y*   (4, *y*), (2, *y*), (5, *y*), (*x*, 13)   <u>10,   </u>

❷ *x* ⟶ (×3) ⟶ *y*   (1, *y*), (2, *y*), (4, *y*), (*x*, 9)   <u>.   </u>

❸ *x* ⟶ (−7) ⟶ *y*   (10, *y*), (15, *y*), (*x*, 0), (*x*, 4)   _____

❹ *x* ⟶ (÷2) ⟶ *y*   (14, *y*), (8, *y*), (*x*, 3), (*x*, 5)   _____

❺ *x* ⟶ (+10) ⟶ *y*   (0, *y*), (*x*, 12), (4, *y*), (*x*, 16)   _____

❻ *x* ⟶ (×1) ⟶ *y*   (1, *y*), (*x*, 3), (5, *y*), (*x*, 10)   _____

Complete each chart. Then graph each set of ordered pairs.

1 $x \rightarrow (\times 8) \rightarrow y$

x	y
0	
2	
4	
5	
6	

2 $x \rightarrow (\div 5) \rightarrow y$

x	y
60	
50	
40	
30	
20	

3 $x \rightarrow (+10) \rightarrow y$

x	y
5	
10	
15	
20	
25	

4 $x \rightarrow (-10) \rightarrow y$

x	y
50	
40	
30	
20	
10	

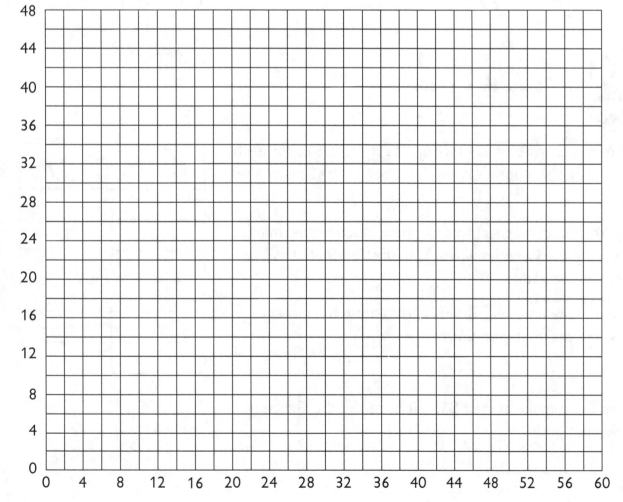

Name_____

Find the value of y.

1 7 →(+2)→ n →(×5)→ y   y = _____

2 30 →(÷6)→ n →(×7)→ y   y = _____

3 12 →(−6)→ n →(÷3)→ y   y = _____

4 18 →(−8)→ n →(+4)→ y   y = _____

5 21 →(−1)→ n →(×0)→ y   y = _____

6 45 →(÷5)→ n →(×4)→ y   y = _____

7 9 →(+10)→ n →(−4)→ y   y = _____

8 8 →(×7)→ n →(−6)→ y   y = _____

9 8 →(×7)→ n →(÷8)→ y   y = _____

10 12 →(÷6)→ n →(+9)→ y   y = _____

11 15 →(−5)→ n →(×9)→ y   y = _____

12 34 →(−12)→ n →(÷2)→ y   y = _____

Solve these problems.

Brian mows lawns to make money. He charges $10 for each time he mows someone's lawn plus a one-time start-up fee of $5.

13 Make a function chart to show how much he will make mowing the Greenes' lawn. The function chart has been started for you.

14 How many times will Brian need to mow the Greenes' lawn to make at least $50?

_____

15 Can Brian make at least $100 if he mows the Greenes' lawn ten times?

_____

x →(×?)→ n →(+?)→ y

x	y
1	15
2	
3	
4	
5	
10	

Name_____

Find the value of x.

1 x —(×2)→ n —(×6)→ 36   x = _____

2 x —(×2)→ n —(+10)→ 16   x = _____

3 x —(+5)→ n —(÷2)→ 7   x = _____

4 x —(+5)→ n —(−9)→ 0   x = _____

5 x —(÷6)→ n —(×3)→ 27   x = _____

6 x —(÷4)→ n —(−2)→ 0   x = _____

7 x —(+5)→ n —(÷4)→ 5   x = _____

8 x —(−9)→ n —(×8)→ 72   x = _____

9 x —(÷10)→ n —(×8)→ 40   x = _____

10 x —(×7)→ n —(−20)→ 22   x = _____

11 x —(×7)→ n —(−8)→ 20   x = _____

12 x —(+10)→ n —(×10)→ 100   x = _____

13 x —(×6)→ n —(÷6)→ 6   x = _____

14 x —(÷7)→ n —(×7)→ 49   x = _____

15 x —(÷7)→ n —(×3)→ 21   x = _____

16 x —(−11)→ n —(÷4)→ 1   x = _____

17 x —(÷6)→ n —(×9)→ 45   x = _____

18 x —(×3)→ n —(×9)→ 81   x = _____

Solve these problems.

19 Three students are absent from Kathleen's ballet class today.
The students who are at class are divided into four groups of
three students each.

   a. How many students are at ballet class today?   _____

   b. How many students are in the class when no one is absent?   _____

Name

Use inverse operations to replace x with the correct number.
Graph each set of ordered pairs.

1 x —(×3)→ y   (x, 6), (x, 15), (x, 30), (x, 0), (x, 24)   _____

2 x —(+6)→ y   (x, 10), (x, 16), (x, 26), (x, 6), (x, 24)   _____

3 x —(−8)→ y   (x, 8), (x, 16), (x, 4), (x, 2), (x, 5)   _____

4 x —(÷2)→ y   (x, 6), (x, 7), (x, 9), (x, 10), (x, 5)   _____

5 x —(×2)→ n —(+6)→ y   (x, 8), (x, 10), (x, 12), (x, 20)   _____

6 x —(÷4)→ n —(−4)→ y   (x, 2), (x, 4), (x, 1), (x, 3)   _____

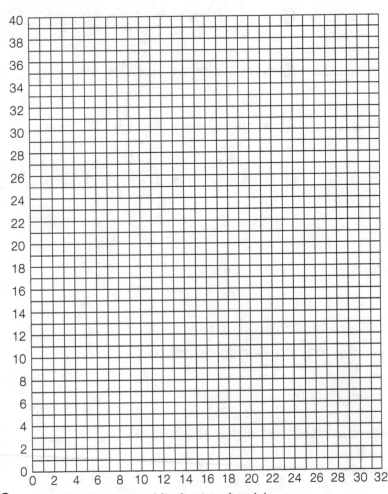

Solve for *n*. Watch the signs.

1 $n + 7 = 17$ _____

2 $n - 20 = 33$ _____

3 $n \div 4 = 8$ _____

4 $63 \div n = 7$ _____

5 $6 \times 3 = n$ _____

6 $n + 8 = 27$ _____

Add or subtract.

7
$$\begin{array}{r} 1478 \\ + 2496 \\ \hline \end{array}$$

8
$$\begin{array}{r} 344 \\ - 129 \\ \hline \end{array}$$

9
$$\begin{array}{r} 1820 \\ + 2688 \\ \hline \end{array}$$

10
$$\begin{array}{r} \$4.06 \\ - 1.68 \\ \hline \end{array}$$

11
$$\begin{array}{r} \$13.56 \\ + 6.64 \\ \hline \end{array}$$

Answer the following questions.

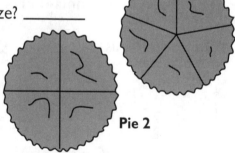

Pie 1

Pie 2

12 Which pie has been cut into pieces that are $\frac{1}{4}$ its size? _____

13 Which pie has been cut into pieces that are $\frac{1}{5}$ its size? _____

14 Which pie has more pieces? _____

15 Which pie has bigger pieces? _____

Solve for *n*. Watch the signs.

16 $n = 9 + 7$ _____

17 $n \times 8 = 56$ _____

18 $n \div 10 = 9$ _____

19 $n = 8 \times 8$ _____

20 $40 \div n = 8$ _____

21 $n - 9 = 29$ _____

22 $6 + n = 25$ _____

23 $n \div 3 = 7$ _____

24 $28 = 7 \times n$ _____

Add or subtract.

25
$$\begin{array}{r} 43 \\ + 9 \\ \hline \end{array}$$

26
$$\begin{array}{r} 43 \\ - 9 \\ \hline \end{array}$$

27
$$\begin{array}{r} 73 \\ - 28 \\ \hline \end{array}$$

28
$$\begin{array}{r} 334 \\ - 83 \\ \hline \end{array}$$

29
$$\begin{array}{r} 425 \\ + 700 \\ \hline \end{array}$$

30
$$\begin{array}{r} 4126 \\ - 2427 \\ \hline \end{array}$$

31
$$\begin{array}{r} 4000 \\ - 1997 \\ \hline \end{array}$$

32
$$\begin{array}{r} \$5.06 \\ + 3.04 \\ \hline \end{array}$$

33
$$\begin{array}{r} \$41.07 \\ - 19.28 \\ \hline \end{array}$$

34
$$\begin{array}{r} \$ 4.07 \\ + 26.93 \\ \hline \end{array}$$

Name_____

For each function rule, follow these steps.

Step 1 Find four ordered pairs of numbers.
Step 2 Graph the four points.
Step 3 Try to draw a line through all four points.

❶ $x \longrightarrow \boxed{\div 1} \longrightarrow y$

❷ $x \longrightarrow \boxed{-5} \longrightarrow y$

_____

_____

❸ $x \longrightarrow \boxed{\div 2} \longrightarrow n \longrightarrow \boxed{+4} \longrightarrow y$

❹ $x \longrightarrow \boxed{\times 2} \longrightarrow y$

_____

_____

For each graph find a function rule.

❺ A function rule is _____.

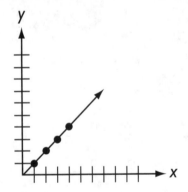

❻ A function rule is _____.

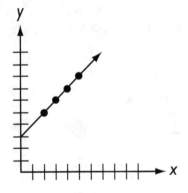

❼ A function rule is _____.

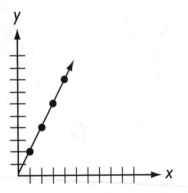

❽ A function rule is _____.

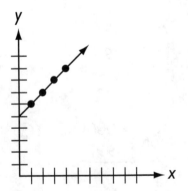

Alexa keeps a record of the books she sells in her bookstore each month. Then she prints a bar graph to show her employees.

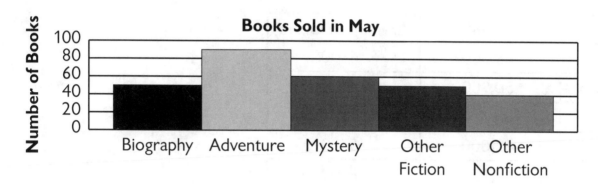

Books Sold in May

Use the bar graph to answer questions 1–3.

❶ How many mystery books were sold this month? _____

❷ For which two types of books were the same number of books sold? _____

❸ For which type of book was the most copies sold? _____

The sporting goods store made a line graph to show the number of sales for the first six months of the year.

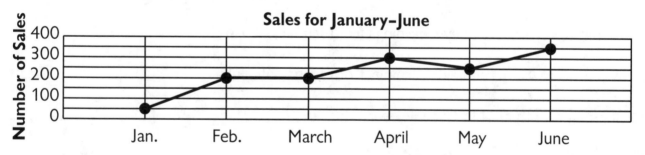

Sales for January–June

Use the line graph to answer questions 4–6.

❹ During which month was the number of sales greatest? _____

❺ During which month was the number of sales least? _____

❻ How many sales were there in April? _____

Name_____

Mr. Greenley owns Computers Are Fun, Inc. The chart below shows
the sales and earnings for the first seven months he was in business.

Year	Sales (Dollars)	Earnings (Dollars)
January	63,500	6300
February	50,900	4750
March	50,750	4500
April	62,000	5700
May	69,350	3100
June	74,725	5900
July	76,200	4900

**Answer the following questions using the information
in the chart. You may use a calculator.**

❶ Make graphs of the sales and earnings for Computers Are Fun,
Inc. over the first seven months. _____

❷ What were Mr. Greenley's earnings from January to April? _____

❸ What were Mr. Greenley's earnings from January to July? _____

❹ In what month did Mr. Greenley earn the most? _____

❺ In which month were sales the least? _____

❻ How much did sales decrease from January to February? _____

❼ Make a graph for earnings that shows the change in earnings
more fairly. _____

Solve for *n*. Watch the signs.

1. $72 \div n = 9$ _____
2. $18 \div 6 = n$ _____
3. $7 \times n = 0$ _____
4. $n - 5 = 8$ _____
5. $8 \times n = 24$ _____
6. $n + 6 = 12$ _____
7. $6 \times 5 = n$ _____
8. $9 - 6 = n$ _____
9. $36 \div 9 = n$ _____
10. $n + 8 = 15$ _____
11. $8 + n = 16$ _____
12. $7 \times n = 63$ _____
13. $17 - n = 8$ _____
14. $4 \times n = 20$ _____
15. $17 - 8 = n$ _____
16. $36 \div 4 = n$ _____
17. $56 \div n = 8$ _____
18. $n \times 8 = 32$ _____
19. $7 + 9 = n$ _____
20. $17 - n = 9$ _____
21. $42 \div n = 7$ _____
22. $4 \times n = 32$ _____
23. $7 \times n = 35$ _____
24. $3 + n = 11$ _____
25. $42 \div 6 = n$ _____
26. $64 \div n = 8$ _____
27. $n - 7 = 8$ _____
28. $n + 6 = 15$ _____
29. $9 + n = 18$ _____
30. $9 + 7 = n$ _____
31. $25 \div n = 5$ _____
32. $10 - n = 4$ _____
33. $9 \times 9 = n$ _____
34. $6 + n = 10$ _____
35. $17 + 0 = n$ _____
36. $54 \div n = 6$ _____
37. $8 - n = 5$ _____
38. $20 \div n = 5$ _____
39. $n - 9 = 10$ _____
40. $n \div 8 = 6$ _____
41. $7 \times n = 21$ _____
42. $9 \times n = 45$ _____
43. $7 + 7 = n$ _____
44. $18 - 9 = n$ _____
45. $n \div 9 = 3$ _____
46. $9 \times n = 27$ _____
47. $7 + n = 15$ _____
48. $8 - 8 = n$ _____
49. $n \times 6 = 54$ _____
50. $63 \div n = 7$ _____
51. $7 \times n = 35$ _____
52. $8 - n = 3$ _____
53. $3 \times n = 27$ _____
54. $10 + n = 15$ _____
55. $n \div 9 = 8$ _____
56. $n - 4 = 9$ _____
57. $n \times 6 = 48$ _____
58. $n + 7 = 14$ _____
59. $60 \div n = 10$ _____
60. $15 - 7 = n$ _____
61. $5 \times 0 = n$ _____
62. $10 + 7 = n$ _____
63. $50 \div 1 = n$ _____

Name_____

Name the following items.

1 *P* is a _____.

2 This is a _____.   A   B

3 *CD* is a _____.   C   D

4 This is a _____.   E   F

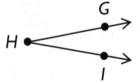

5 This is an _____.

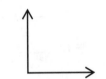

6 This is a _____ angle.

Answer the following questions.

7 How many lines can go through two points? _____

8 If two lines meet at point *P*, can they meet at another point? _____

9 Is an angle made up of two rays? _____

Name each shape.

10  _____   **11** _____   **12** 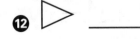 _____

LESSON
69
PRACTICE

Name_____

In each case tell whether the two lines are *parallel*, *perpendicular*, or *neither*.

1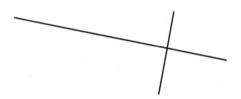

_____

2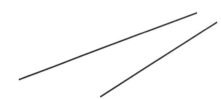

_____

3

_____

4

_____

Identify the quadrilateral as a *parallelogram*, *rectangle*, *rhombus*, *square*, or *trapezoid*.

5 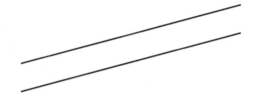 _____

6 _____

7 _____

8 _____

9 _____

10  _____

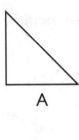
A

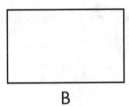
B

C

D

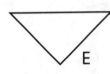
E

F

G

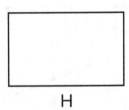
H

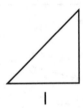
I

J

Answer the following questions.

1 Which figures are congruent to A? _____

2 Which figures are similar to A? _____

3 Which figures are congruent to B? _____

4 Which figures are similar to B? _____

5 Which figures are similar to I? _____

Consider these rectangles. Answer the following questions.

6 Are they similar? _____

7 Are they congruent? _____

8 Do they have the same area? _____

Fill in the blanks. Write whether each figure is a *reflection*, *rotation*, or *translation*.

A   B   C   D

1 B is a _____ of A.

2 C is a _____ of A.

3 D is a _____ of A.

E   F   G   H

4 F is a _____ of E.

5 G is a _____ of E.

6 H is a _____ of E.

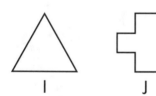

I   J

Answer the following questions.

7 Is I congruent to E? _____

8 Is J congruent to A? _____

9 What figures are congruent to A? _____

10 What figures are congruent to E? _____

Name the figure.

1

_____

2

_____

3

_____

4

_____

5

_____

6

_____

What figure can you make with the following nets?

7

_____

8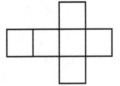

_____

9

_____

10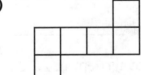

_____

Name_____

Trace the figures. Then find out how many lines of symmetry there are in each.

❶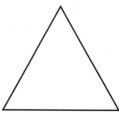

_____

❷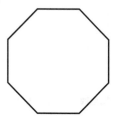

_____

❸

_____

❹

_____

❺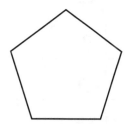

_____

❻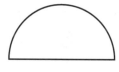

_____

❼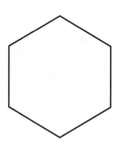

_____

❽

_____

❾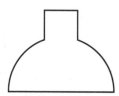

_____

Answer the following questions.

❿ Can parallel lines be used to divide line segments into equal parts? _____

⓫ If you want to divide a line segment into five equal parts, how many parallel lines will you need? _____

Name_____

A
1 cm ▭
2 cm

B
2 cm ▭
4 cm

C
3 cm ▭
6 cm

D
4 cm ▭
8 cm

Consider the similar rectangles above. Complete the chart.

Rectangle	Perimeter	Area
A	**1**	**2**
B	**3**	**4**
C	**5**	**6**
D	**7**	**8**

Use your chart to answer the questions below.

9 As you double the length of the sides, what happens to the perimeter? _____

10 As you double the length of the sides, what happens to the area? _____

11 As you triple the length of the sides, what happens to the perimeter? _____

12 As you triple the length of the sides, what happens to the area? _____

13 As you multiply the length of the sides by 4, what happens to the perimeter? _____

14 As you multiply the length of the sides by 4, what happens to the area? _____

Name_____

Look at the graph. What are the coordinates of these points?

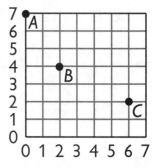

1 A _____

2 B _____

3 C _____

Find the value of *x* or *y*.

4 $x \longrightarrow \boxed{+7} \longrightarrow 15$

x = _____

5 $14 \longrightarrow \boxed{-6} \longrightarrow n \longrightarrow \boxed{\times 3} \longrightarrow y$

y = _____

Solve for *n*.

6 $56 \div n = 7$ _____

7 $6 \times n = 30$ _____

8 $n + 7 = 20$ _____

9 $n - 7 = 16$ _____

10 $8 + n = 27$ _____

11 $25 - n = 16$ _____

Add or subtract. Watch the signs.

12
```
  847
+ 793
```

13
```
  584
-  98
```

14
```
326,398
- 22,509
```

15
```
 83,218
+ 15,647
```

Solve this problem.

16 Susan saves $5 a month. How long will it take her to save $40? _____

Tell whether each angle is a right angle. Write *yes* or *no*.

17

_____

18

_____

Name_____

What is the value of y?

1 17 ——(+8)——▶ y

y = _____

2 19 ——(−6)——▶ y

y = _____

3 6 ——(×8)——▶ y

y = _____

4 32 ——(÷4)——▶ y

y = _____

5 4 ——(+15)——▶ y

y = _____

6 20 ——(−10)——▶ y

y = _____

What is the value of x?

7 x ——(−7)——▶ 0

x = _____

8 x ——(÷3)——▶ 7

x = _____

9 x ——(+5)——▶ 25

x = _____

10 x ——(×1)——▶ 44

x = _____

11 x ——(−12)——▶ 59

x = _____

12 x ——(×9)——▶ 63

x = _____

Give a possible function rule for each set of ordered pairs.

13

x ——( )——▶ y

x	y
1	6
4	9
8	13

14

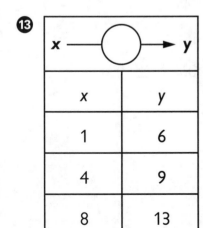

x ——( )——▶ y

x	y
12	4
18	6
30	10

15

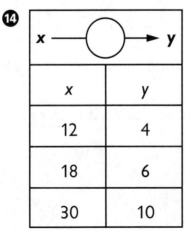

x ——( )——▶ y

x	y
7	14
5	10
10	20

LESSON 77 PRACTICE

Name_____

Solve for *n*. Watch the signs.

1 $16 - n = 9$

n = _____

2 $42 \div 7 = n$

n = _____

3 $n = 8 \times 6$

n = _____

4 $n = 5 + 15$

n = _____

Add or subtract.

5
```
  641
- 245
```

6
```
  646
+ 406
```

7
```
  158
+ 779
```

8
```
  7376
- 6289
```

9
```
  156
+ 179
```

Tell whether each angle is a right angle. Write *yes* or *no*.

10 ____

11 ____

12 ____

13 ____

Tell whether the lines are *parallel, perpendicular,* or *neither*.

14  _____

15  _____

How many lines of symmetry can be drawn in each figure?

16 ____

17 ____

18 ____

19 ____

 **Solve this problem.**

20 Jessica rides her bike 8 miles every day. How many days will it take her to ride a total of 72 miles?

_____

Multiply.

1 $100 \times 5 =$ _____

2 $89 \times 10 =$ _____

3 $10 \times 10 =$ _____

4 $6 \times 1000 =$ _____

5 $1000 \times 6 =$ _____

6 $41 \times 10,000 =$ _____

7 $1000 \times 8 =$ _____

8 $12 \times 10 =$ _____

9 $80 \times 10 =$ _____

10 $50 \times 100 =$ _____

11 $421 \times 10 =$ _____

12 $81 \times 1000 =$ _____

13 $824 \times 100 =$ _____

14 $64 \times 10 =$ _____

15 $1000 \times 417 =$ _____

16 $6 \times 10,000 =$ _____

17 $100 \times 10 =$ _____

18 $608 \times 100 =$ _____

19 $98 \times 100 =$ _____

20 $137 \times 1000 =$ _____

21 $10 \times 2731 =$ _____

22 $75 \times 10,000 =$ _____

23 $1000 \times 86 =$ _____

24 $11 \times 100 =$ _____

25 $31 \times 100 =$ _____

26 $307 \times 10 =$ _____

27 $18 \times 10,000 =$ _____

28 $8 \times 1000 =$ _____

29 $49 \times 100 =$ _____

30 $89 \times 10,000 =$ _____

31 $14 \times 10 =$ _____

32 $100 \times 100 =$ _____

33 $138 \times 100 =$ _____

34 $10 \times 10,000 =$ _____

35 $7 \times 1000 =$ _____

36 $1000 \times 1000 =$ _____

37 $246 \times 10 =$ _____

38 $1,000,000 \times 10 =$ _____

39 $48 \times 100 =$ _____

40 $4000 \times 1000 =$ _____

41 $167 \times 10,000 =$ _____

42 $10 \times 100 =$ _____

Name_____

Answer the following questions.

Remember: 1 meter = 100 centimeters, and 1000 meters = 1 kilometer

1 How many centimeters are there in 6 meters? _____

2 How many meters are there in 6 kilometers? _____

3 How many centimeters are there in 62 meters? _____

4 How many centimeters are there in 10 meters? _____

5 How many meters are there in 62 kilometers? _____

6 How many meters are there in 10 kilometers? _____

Remember: 1000 milliliters = 1 liter

7 How many milliliters are there in 6 liters? _____

8 How many milliliters are there in 62 liters? _____

9 Six dollars is worth how many cents? _____

10 How many cents is $62? _____

11 How many grams are there in 6 kilograms? _____

12 How many grams are there in 62 kilograms? _____

James rode his bike all day. At the end of the day he said, "I rode 15 kilometers."

13 Do you think James could have ridden 15 kilometers? _____

14 How far is that in centimeters? _____

Multiply.

1. $60 \times 4 = $ _____

2. $60 \times 60 = $ _____

3. $6 \times 40 = $ _____

4. $8 \times 80 = $ _____

5. $60 \times 40 = $ _____

6. $90 \times 300 = $ _____

7. $600 \times 400 = $ _____

8. $20 \times 50 = $ _____

9. $6000 \times 4000 = $ _____

10. $8 \times 900 = $ _____

11. $30 \times 700 = $ _____

12. $600 \times 700 = $ _____

13. $80 \times 4000 = $ _____

14. $300 \times 90 = $ _____

15. $9 \times 800 = $ _____

16. $6 \times 9000 = $ _____

17. $70 \times 5000 = $ _____

18. $40 \times 500 = $ _____

19. $400 \times 700 = $ _____

20. $7 \times 700 = $ _____

21. $8 \times 3000 = $ _____

22. $2 \times 3000 = $ _____

23. $60 \times 7000 = $ _____

24. $50 \times 50 = $ _____

25. $800 \times 5 = $ _____

26. $8 \times 40 = $ _____

27. $7000 \times 60 = $ _____

28. $9 \times 200 = $ _____

29. $50 \times 300 = $ _____

30. $400 \times 80 = $ _____

31. $9 \times 5000 = $ _____

32. $90 \times 7000 = $ _____

33. $90 \times 90 = $ _____

34. $20 \times 60 = $ _____

35. $600 \times 300 = $ _____

36. $8 \times 60 = $ _____

37. $70 \times 8000 = $ _____

38. $30 \times 4000 = $ _____

39. $6 \times 50 = $ _____

40. $9 \times 600 = $ _____

41. $30 \times 30 = $ _____

42. $4 \times 700 = $ _____

Multiply.

1 10 × 100 = _____

2 10 × 10,000 = _____

3 100 × 100 = _____

4 10,000 × 10,000 = _____

5 10,000 × 10 = _____

6 100 × 1000 = _____

7 1000 × 1000 = _____

8 1000 × 10 = _____

9 100,000 × 100 = _____

10 10,000 × 1000 = _____

11 20 × 20 = _____

12 1000 × 600 = _____

13 400 × 100 = _____

14 200 × 800 = _____

15 1000 × 30 = _____

16 70 × 70 = _____

17 800 × 300 = _____

18 9000 × 10,000 = _____

19 17 × 10 = _____

20 40,000 × 5000 = _____

21 704 × 100 = _____

22 60 × 700 = _____

23 328 × 1000 = _____

24 6000 × 6000 = _____

25 50,000 × 600 = _____

26 10,000 × 740 = _____

27 808 × 10 = _____

28 90 × 60 = _____

29 72 × 10 = _____

30 280 × 700 = _____

Answer the following questions.

31 There are 10 centimeters in a decimeter and 10 decimeters in a meter. How many centimeters are there in a meter? _____

32 How many centimeters are there in 6 meters? _____

33 There are 1000 meters in a kilometer. How many meters are there in 5 kilometers? _____

Approximate to solve these problems.

1 Ken needs $10.00. He has six jars of fishing worms he can sell for $1.95 each. If he sells all six jars, will he have at least $10.00? _____

2 The students at Kennedy School need 2000 soup labels to win a prize for the school. If each of the six classes turns in about 200 labels, will they have enough to win the prize? _____

3 Lian wants to buy ten apples that cost 10¢ each. Does she have enough money if she has exactly $1.10? _____

4 Ricardo is eight years old. Is he more than 5000 days old? _____

5 A baseball stadium has 50 rows of seats with 420 seats in a row. Will the stadium hold at least 2000 people? _____

6 At a basketball game Pam sells large bags of popcorn for 75¢ each. If she sells 200 bags, will she take in at least $200? _____

7 Doug wants to buy 200 sheets of paper that are sold at 45¢ for a packet of 50. Will $1.50 cover the cost of 200 sheets? _____

8 JoAnn wants to run 250 kilometers each month. Can she do this by running 6 kilometers each day? _____

9 Claire earns $9.00 an hour working at a store. If she works ten hours, will she have earned enough money to buy a watch that costs $80.00? _____

For each statement choose the most appropriate answer.
Use each answer only once.

10 **a.** The plane will arrive _____   1. at around 12:00.

 b. Chris is coming to lunch _____   2. at 12:04.

 c. The timed math test ended _____   3. at 12:04 and 30 seconds.

**In each problem two of the answers are clearly wrong and one
is correct. Choose the correct answer.**

1 $42 \times 16 =$ _____   **a.** 342   **b.** 672   **c.** 1912

2 $12 \times 37 =$ _____   **a.** 444   **b.** 682   **c.** 1042

3 $84 \times 61 =$ _____   **a.** 2824   **b.** 5124   **c.** 3512

4 $92 \times 59 =$ _____   **a.** 6418   **b.** 829   **c.** 5428

5 $702 \times 48 =$ _____   **a.** 2839   **b.** 432,142   **c.** 33,696

6 $32 \times 645 =$ _____   **a.** 20,640   **b.** 2140   **c.** 200,740

7 $602 \times 501 =$ _____   **a.** 540,212   **b.** 301,602   **c.** 721,800

8 $45 \times 66 =$ _____   **a.** 1970   **b.** 2970   **c.** 3970

9 $1402 \times 76 =$ _____   **a.** 1,841,200   **b.** 10,500   **c.** 106,552

10 $8447 \times 340 =$ _____   **a.** 2,871,980   **b.** 1,000,847   **c.** 4,200,500

11 $122 \times 333 =$ _____   **a.** 40,626   **b.** 562,406   **c.** 4250

12 $999 \times 27 =$ _____   **a.** 4842   **b.** 36,823   **c.** 26,973

13 $201 \times 55 =$ _____   **a.** 11,055   **b.** 9050   **c.** 152,005

14 $562 \times 26 =$ _____   **a.** 8142   **b.** 34,006   **c.** 14,612

15 $904 \times 878 =$ _____   **a.** 427,282   **b.** 793,712   **c.** 127,602

16 $709 \times 75 =$ _____   **a.** 65,175   **b.** 43,175   **c.** 53,175

17 $87 \times 39 =$ _____   **a.** 3393   **b.** 3893   **c.** 2093

18 $31 \times 31 =$ _____   **a.** 691   **b.** 961   **c.** 1331

19 $201 \times 79 =$ _____   **a.** 15,879   **b.** 25,879   **c.** 35,879

20 $35 \times 53 =$ _____   **a.** 1455   **b.** 1855   **c.** 1055

Name_____

Complete the chart below. Approximate the answer to each problem using scientific notation. Then use your calculator to find the answer. Comment on whether you could have made a better approximation for each problem.

	Standard Form	Approximation	Answer	Comment
1	756×763			
2	$68,589 \times 7,496$			
3	$550 \times 85,000$			
4	5496×6498			
5	12×4490			
6	$200,000 \times 30,000$			
7	39×41			
8	699×31			
9	545×649			
10	800×900			

Name_____

Multiply. Use shortcuts when you can.

1　　35
　　× 3

2　　19
　　× 7

3　　46
　　× 5

4　　62
　　× 2

5　　74
　　× 3

6　　76
　　× 8

7　　91
　　× 9

8　　59
　　× 6

9　　73
　　× 5

10　　43
　　× 4

11　　85
　　× 4

12　　78
　　× 8

13　　98
　　× 3

14　　49
　　× 6

15　　56
　　× 7

16　　80
　　× 3

17　　45
　　× 7

18　　93
　　× 4

19　　88
　　× 2

20　　89
　　× 3

21　　56
　　× 9

22　　83
　　× 8

23　　38
　　× 7

24　　27
　　× 6

25　　56
　　× 5

26　　36
　　× 9

27　　51
　　× 8

28　　65
　　× 5

29　　83
　　× 2

30　　44
　　× 4

Name_____

Multiply. Use shortcuts when you can.

1 453
× 8

2 400
× 7

3 569
× 5

4 436
× 4

5 585
× 7

6 568
× 3

7 600
× 8

8 382
× 9

9 64
× 6

10 821
× 5

11 521
× 2

12 400
× 9

13 409
× 7

14 401
× 8

15 646
× 7

16 458
× 6

17 88
× 5

18 986
× 6

19 823
× 4

20 85
× 9

21 300
× 4

22 697
× 9

23 689
× 3

24 751
× 8

25 193
× 9

26 505
× 7

27 469
× 6

28 469
× 3

29 200
× 4

30 844
× 2

Name_____

Multiply.

1 65
× 7

2 307
× 3

3 99
× 4

4 615
× 8

5 395
× 2

6 401
× 6

7 443
× 7

8 56
× 3

9 80
× 8

10 406
× 9

11 56 × 7 = _____

12 720 × 9 = _____

13 82 × 6 = _____

14 28 × 7 = _____

15 15 × 3 = _____

16 107 × 4 = _____

17 91 × 8 = _____

18 630 × 2 = _____

19 92 × 6 = _____

20 321 × 5 = _____

21 444 × 4 = _____

22 850 × 3 = _____

Solve these problems.

23 Mary jogs 5 kilometers every day. How far does she jog in 15 days? _____

24 Solomon gets eight football cards in every pack of gum he buys. How many cards will he get if he buys seven packs? _____

25 Thomas is packing supplies for a camping trip. He will make pancakes four times. He will use three packages of pancake mix each time he makes pancakes. How many packages of pancake mix should he pack? _____

26 A plane traveled at a speed of 600 miles per hour for four hours. How many miles did the plane travel? _____

27 Sonja's car travels 20 miles on 1 gallon of gasoline. How far can she go on 9 gallons of gasoline? _____

Name_____

Multiply. Use shortcuts when you can.

1 27
 × 5

2 91
 × 8

3 72
 × 7

4 43
 × 6

5 78
 × 74

6 18
 × 20

7 43
 × 40

8 47
 × 48

9 80
 × 80

10 64
 × 13

11 99
 × 34

12 95
 × 36

13 28
 × 46

14 21
 × 89

15 65
 × 87

16 91
 × 24

17 53
 × 27

18 92
 × 28

19 69
 × 15

20 77
 × 77

Solve these problems.

21 Ann is setting up chairs for the assembly. She knows that there are 525 students in the school. She sets up chairs in rows of 25.

a. Will 20 rows be too few, just enough, or too many? _____

b. If only 498 students are present that day, how many extra seats are there (in 20 rows of 25 chairs)? _____

LESSON 89 PRACTICE

Name_____

Solve these problems.

1 Jim bought five folders that cost 78¢ each, including tax.
  a. How much did the five folders cost all together?

  _____

  b. If Jim gave the cashier $5.00, how much change would he get back?

  _____

2 Ruth is knitting a scarf. She needs 98 pieces of yarn that are each 3 meters long. Will 250 meters of yarn be enough?

  _____

3 If seven children each weigh 35 kilograms, do they weigh more than 200 kilograms all together?

  _____

4 A rectangle is 52 centimeters long and 36 centimeters wide.
  a. What is its area?

  _____

  b. What is its perimeter?

  _____

5 Juan needs to buy 12 cans of soda, four loaves of bread, and two packages of cheese. The soda is 50¢ a can; the bread is 90¢ a loaf; and the cheese is $1.50 a package. Will $20 be enough money for him to buy what he needs?

  _____

6 Name the polygons you can find in the diagram below.

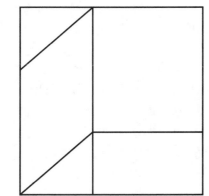

  a. _____ **b.** _____

  c. _____ **d.** _____

  e. _____ **f.** _____

  g. _____

Name_____

Multiply. Use shortcuts when you can.

1   32
     × 46

2   84
     × 21

3   45
     × 16

4   58
     × 37

5   83
     × 94

6   72
     × 30

7   67
     × 56

8   25
     × 38

9   49
     × 29

10   60
     × 50

11   29
     × 18

12   79
     × 64

13   26
     × 21

14   17
     × 15

15   64
     × 63

Choose the answer that is most reasonable for the following multiplication problems.

16 $82 \times 37 =$ _____   **a.** 3034   **b.** 2418   **c.** 30,304

17 $53 \times 53 =$ _____   **a.** 28,009   **b.** 2806   **c.** 2809

18 $40 \times 62 =$ _____   **a.** 248   **b.** 2480   **c.** 102

19 $74 \times 45 =$ _____   **a.** 280   **b.** 3330   **c.** 33,000

20 $92 \times 80 =$ _____   **a.** 736   **b.** 7216   **c.** 7360

Name_____

Multiply. Use shortcuts when you can. Check to see that your answers make sense.

1 247 × 42	**2** 561 × 59	**3** 412 × 65	**4** 256 × 32	**5** 425 × 27

6 706 × 36	**7** 161 × 7	**8** 161 × 70	**9** 334 × 8	**10** 334 × 80

11 45 × 27	**12** 450 × 27	**13** 8 × 8	**14** 80 × 8	**15** 800 × 8

16 80 × 80	**17** 800 × 80	**18** 5 × 7	**19** 50 × 70	**20** 500 × 70

21 642 × 27	**22** 984 × 31	**23** 758 × 16	**24** 214 × 5	**25** 488 × 69

26 785 × 61	**27** 290 × 10	**28** 85 × 56	**29** 274 × 75	**30** 85 × 84

Answer these questions.

1 How many ounces are there in 12 pounds? _____

2 How many pounds are there in 320 ounces? _____

3 How many inches are there in 5 feet? _____

4 How many inches are there in 5 yards? _____

5 How many feet are there in 11 yards? _____

6 How many feet are there in 96 inches? _____

7 How many pints are there in 8 gallons? _____

8 How many quarts are there in 8 gallons? _____

Solve these problems.

9 Mr. Wong bought 6 feet of wood. He cut off a piece that was 18 inches long. How many feet of wood does he have left? _____

10 Stella bought a gallon of milk. Her family drank 56 ounces for breakfast. How many ounces of milk are left? _____

11 Mrs. Finn bought $3\frac{3}{4}$ yards of fabric. Mrs. Pine bought 13 feet of fabric. Who bought more fabric? _____

12 Marge bought pints of ice cream for a party. She bought 1 pint of strawberry, 3 pints of chocolate, and 3 pints of vanilla. Did she buy a gallon of ice cream all together? _____

13 Mrs. Smith is baking brownies. She bought a 5-pound bag of sugar. The recipe called for 8 ounces of sugar. Mrs. Smith is making four batches of brownies. How many ounces of sugar will she have left? _____

Name_____

If you know that the length of a rectangle is 394 meters and the width is 22 meters, you can approximate the area by multiplying 400×20. Your estimate would be 8000 square meters. The exact area is 8668 square meters.

Approximate the answers to these problems. Then use your calculator to find the precise answers. Compare these answers with your approximated answers.

1 389×61 _____, _____

2 52×777 _____, _____

3 51×597 _____, _____

4 89×73 _____, _____

5 98×305 _____, _____

6 101×41 _____, _____

7 35×352 _____, _____

8 74×163 _____, _____

9 87×754 _____, _____

10 63×77 _____, _____

11 256×12 _____, _____

12 75×234 _____, _____

13 26×136 _____, _____

14 58×30 _____, _____

15 29×34 _____, _____

16 23×46 _____, _____

17 16×140 _____, _____

18 27×276 _____, _____

Solve these problems.

The drama club decided to sell candy bars to raise money. Each box of candy bars contains 20 candy bars. The drama club must pay $10 for each box and must buy at least ten boxes.

19 The drama club members decide to charge $1 per candy bar. If they buy ten boxes and sell all ten boxes, will they make a profit? How much? _____

20 If they buy ten boxes, how many candy bars will they have to sell to break even? Give the answer in candy bars and boxes. _____

Multiply. Use shortcuts when you can.

1   258
      × 325

2   604
      × 283

3   912
      × 456

4   278
      × 61

5   823
      × 649

6   925
      × 683

7   264
      × 172

8   808
      × 27

9   987
      ×   8

10   548
       ×   7

11   295
       × 592

12   703
       × 333

**Below are four multiplication problems that have been worked
out. Two of them have errors. Ring the numbers that are errors.
Write *correct* below the problems that are correct.**

13   3 3 5
        ×   5 7
        ———————
          2 3 4 5
        1 6 7 5
        ———————
        1 9, 0 9 5

14   7 2 8
        × 6 2 7
        ———————
          5 0 9 6
        1 4 5 6
        4 3 6 8
        ———————
        4 5 6, 4 5 6

15   4 1 9
        × 3 0 7
        ———————
          2 8 6 3
        1 2 5 7 0
        ———————
        1 2 8, 5 6 3

16   5 4 9
        × 1 2 6
        ———————
          3 2 9 5
        1 0 8 8
        5 4 9
        ———————
        6 9, 0 7 4

Solve these problems.

Janelle's club is making and selling doll blankets. Each blanket requires a rectangular piece of fabric 15 inches long and 10 inches wide. The members of the club buy the fabric in large pieces that are 75 inches long and 50 inches wide.

1 Draw a picture to find out how many doll blankets they can make from one large piece of fabric. How many blankets can they make? _____

2 Janelle's club bought ten pieces of fabric. How many doll blankets can the club members make? _____

3 Each large piece of fabric cost $9.98 (998 cents), including tax. How much did the club members pay for the ten large pieces of fabric they bought? _____

4 The club members sold each doll blanket for $4.00, and they sold all of them. How much money did the club take in? _____

5 The club also paid for other supplies besides the fabric. The other supplies cost $10.20 all together. How much profit did the club make? _____

6 The next month the fabric they bought was on sale for $8.50 (850 cents), including tax. They bought 20 large pieces of fabric. How much did they pay? _____

7 How many doll blankets can they make from these 20 large pieces of fabric? _____

8 The club members sold all of these blankets for $3.00 each. How much money did they take in? _____

9 If their other supplies cost $25.00, how much profit did they make? _____

Complete these function machine charts.

1

x ——(+8)—→ y

x	y
0	
6	
	16

2

x ——(−5)—→ y

x	y
10	
	9
20	

3

x ——(×4)—→ y

x	y
20	
10	
0	

Solve for *n*. Watch the signs.

4 $n = 9 + 8$ _____

5 $n = 9 \times 9$ _____

6 $8 \times n = 56$ _____

7 $n \div 10 = 50$ _____

8 $5 + n = 20$ _____

9 $32 \div n = 8$ _____

10 $36 \div 6 = n$ _____

11 $n - 9 = 38$ _____

12 $n \times 6 = 54$ _____

Solve for *n*. Watch the signs.

13 $35 + 13 = n$ _____

14 $35 - 13 = n$ _____

15 $35 \times 13 = n$ _____

16 $417 - 396 = n$ _____

17 $405 \times 35 = n$ _____

18 $428 + 394 = n$ _____

19 $10 \times 24 = n$ _____

20 $156 \times 100 = n$ _____

21 $223 \times 1000 = n$ _____

22 $32 \times 10,000 = n$ _____

Add.

23
```
  37
  39
+ 57
```

24
```
  423
  412
+ 501
```

25
```
  1006
   952
+  228
```

26
```
  15
  28
+ 25
```

27
```
  29
  40
+ 60
```

Name_____

 Solve these problems.

Mr. Garza is buying carpet for his basement. The carpet must be
30 meters long and 24 meters wide. Mr. Johnson is also carpeting
his basement. He must buy carpet that is 42 meters long and
16 meters wide.

Mr. Garza's carpet   Mr. Johnson's carpet

30 m   42 m

24 m   16 m

1 What is the perimeter of Mr. Garza's carpet?   _____

2 What is the perimeter of Mr. Johnson's carpet?   _____

3 What is the area of Mr. Garza's carpet?   _____

4 What is the area of Mr. Johnson's carpet?   _____

Billy and Tim both built pens for their dogs. Billy made a pen
12 meters by 8 meters. Tim's dog has a pen that is 15 meters by
6 meters.

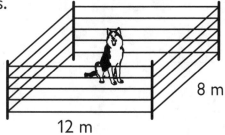

8 m

12 m

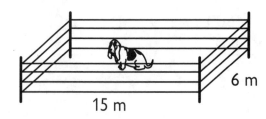

6 m

15 m

5 Who used more fencing to build his dog's pen?   _____

6 How much more fencing was used?   _____

7 What is the area of Billy's dog pen?   _____

8 Whose dog has a larger play area?   _____

Multiply. Use shortcuts when you can.

1   7631
     × 204

2   3700
     ×   16

3   909
     × 475

4   8034
     × 6003

5   6132
     × 5194

6   2483
     × 6195

7   7200
     × 3500

8   27
     ×   53

9   6320
     ×   57

10   795
     ×   90

11   3703
     × 404

12   9603
     × 156

13   408
     × 715

14   2650
     × 830

15   361
     × 872

16   1304
     × 3485

17   4600
     × 3901

18   210
     × 285

19   5036
     × 243

20   7108
     × 4320

21   649
     × 298

22   2851
     × 1649

23   7934
     × 628

24   2740
     × 4919

Name_____

Solve for *n*. Watch the signs.

1 $8 \times 7 = n$

n = ____

2 $9 + 6 = n$

n = ____

3 $10 \times 4 = n$

n = ____

4 $n = 20 \div 5$

n = ____

5 $16 - 9 = n$

n = ____

6 $32 \div 8 = n$

n = ____

7 $n = 9 \times 5$

n = ____

8 $20 - n = 7$

n = ____

9 $n = 6 \times 7$

n = ____

10 $n + 7 = 15$

n = ____

11 $4 \times 6 = n$

n = ____

12 $20 - 4 = n$

n = ____

13 $9 \times 3 = n$

n = ____

14 $n = 10 \div 2$

n = ____

15 $12 - 4 = n$

n = ____

16 $25 \div n = 5$

n = ____

17 $n = 4 \times 3$

n = ____

18 $11 - n = 2$

n = ____

19 $n = 7 \times 7$

n = ____

20 $n + 3 = 13$

n = ____

21 $34 - 6 = n$

n = ____

22 $9 \div 9 = n$

n = ____

23 $n = 10 \times 8$

n = ____

24 $n = 12 - 12$

n = ____

25 $n = 40 \div 5$

n = ____

26 $4 \times 10 = n$

n = ____

27 $24 \div 4 = n$

n = ____

28 $n = 6 \times 5$

n = ____

29 $8 + 8 = n$

n = ____

30 $17 = n + 9$

n = ____

Solve. Watch the signs.

31
$$\begin{array}{r} 37 \\ \times\ 8 \\ \hline \end{array}$$

32
$$\begin{array}{r} 116 \\ +\ 245 \\ \hline \end{array}$$

33
$$\begin{array}{r} 29 \\ \times\ 4 \\ \hline \end{array}$$

34
$$\begin{array}{r} 43 \\ -\ 18 \\ \hline \end{array}$$

35
$$\begin{array}{r} 42 \\ \times\ 7 \\ \hline \end{array}$$

36
$$\begin{array}{r} 248 \\ +\ 723 \\ \hline \end{array}$$

37
$$\begin{array}{r} 835 \\ +\ 516 \\ \hline \end{array}$$

38
$$\begin{array}{r} 365 \\ -\ 209 \\ \hline \end{array}$$

39
$$\begin{array}{r} 33 \\ \times\ 51 \\ \hline \end{array}$$

40
$$\begin{array}{r} 231 \\ -\ 161 \\ \hline \end{array}$$

41
$$\begin{array}{r} 923 \\ -\ 899 \\ \hline \end{array}$$

42
$$\begin{array}{r} 126 \\ +\ 493 \\ \hline \end{array}$$

43
$$\begin{array}{r} 407 \\ -\ 188 \\ \hline \end{array}$$

44
$$\begin{array}{r} 83 \\ \times\ 7 \\ \hline \end{array}$$

45
$$\begin{array}{r} 463 \\ +\ 187 \\ \hline \end{array}$$

Name_____

Solve these problems.

Fred travels about 65 kilometers in one hour on the highway. His van goes about 17 kilometers on 1 liter of gasoline. The gas tank holds 36 liters. Mike drives more slowly. Mike travels about 55 kilometers in one hour on the highway. Mike's car goes about 21 kilometers on 1 liter of gasoline, and his gas tank holds 28 liters.

1 About how far can Fred travel on one tankful of gasoline? _____

2 About how far can Fred travel in four hours on the highway? _____

3 About how far can Mike travel on one tankful of gasoline? _____

4 Who travels farther on one tankful, Fred or Mike? About how much farther? _____

5 Who travels farther in one hour, Fred or Mike? About how much farther? _____

Harold and Samantha have the same kind of car. Harold drives faster. Harold goes 80 kilometers in one hour but he gets only about 14 kilometers to one liter of gasoline. Harold's tank holds 24 liters. Samantha travels about 55 kilometers in one hour but she gets 20 kilometers to one liter of gasoline.

6 About how far does Samantha travel on one tank of gasoline? _____

7 Who travels farther on one tankful, Harold or Samantha? _____

8 Can Samantha make a 1200-kilometer trip on three tankfuls of gasoline? _____

9 Who travels farther in one hour, Harold or Samantha? _____

Name_____

Paint has spilled on this page. Choose the correct answer in each case. Watch the signs.

1   45☐
× 6☐

a. 28,086
b. 2400
c. 260,345

2   43,☐
+   67☐

a. 43,204
b. 4675
c. 44,543

3   ☐
×   ☐0

a. 8323
b. 1405
c. 6900

4   10,36☐
−   1☐

a. 11,467
b. 9120
c. 90,354

5   146
×   4☐

a. 6278
b. 4504
c. 1464

6   85,☐
−   4,5☐

a. 81,132
b. 90,132
c. 8674

7   30,☐
×   24☐

a. 4,380,137
b. 7,380,135
c. 8,124,350

8   ☐73
+ 1☐7

a. ☐045
b. ☐510
c. ☐361

9   8☐6
−   3☐

a. 531
b. 1106
c. 1276

10   ☐85
×   ☐00

a. ☐,400
b. ☐,030
c. ☐0,000

11   ☐000
+   ☐800

a. 200
b. 7800
c. 6400

12   1,632,☐
−   ☐

a. 3,☐
b. 1,☐
c. 10,☐

13   62☐
× 2☐

a. 15,245,395
b. 1,245,395
c. 126,245,395

14   6,42☐
−   ☐

a. 4542
b. 8542
c. 12,422

15   216
× 3☐

a. 5806
b. 7646
c. 76,464

16   4☐5
+ 1☐5

a. ☐1
b. 1☐0
c. 2☐3

Solve for *n*. Watch the signs.

① $n \times 7 = 63$
n = _____

② $9 + n = 45$
n = _____

③ $n \times 4 = 28$
n = _____

④ $8 = n \div 4$
n = _____

⑤ $16 - n = 9$
n = _____

⑥ $45 \div n = 5$
n = _____

⑦ $n = 10 \times 5$
n = _____

⑧ $n - 18 = 41$
n = _____

Multiply. Use shortcuts when you can.

⑨ $12 \times 7 =$ _____

⑩ $70 \times 90 =$ _____

⑪ $312 \times 5 =$ _____

⑫ $146 \times 36 =$ _____

⑬ $3000 \times 40 =$ _____

⑭ $27 \times 84 =$ _____

Solve. Watch the signs.

⑮ 43
  × 18

⑯ 43
  + 18

⑰ 43
  − 18

⑱ 645
  − 519

⑲ 645
  × 519

⑳ 645
  + 519

㉑ 205
  + 836

㉒ 836
  − 205

㉓ 836
  × 205

㉔ 214
  × 14

Solve these problems.

A rectangular garden is 5 meters wide and 12 meters long.

㉕ What is the area of the garden? _____

㉖ What is the perimeter of the garden? _____

Solve for *n*. Watch the signs.

1 $48 + 16 = n$

$n =$ _____

2 $5 \times 8 = n$

$n =$ _____

3 $n + 26 = 84$

$n =$ _____

4 $3 \times n = 27$

$n =$ _____

5 $n - 34 = 9$

$n =$ _____

6 $n \times 9 = 54$

$n =$ _____

7 $39 + n = 76$

$n =$ _____

8 $6 \times n = 30$

$n =$ _____

Multiply.

9
$$\begin{array}{r} 1045 \\ \times \quad 36 \\ \hline \end{array}$$

10
$$\begin{array}{r} 312 \\ \times \ 240 \\ \hline \end{array}$$

11
$$\begin{array}{r} 436 \\ \times \quad 18 \\ \hline \end{array}$$

12
$$\begin{array}{r} 83,625 \\ \times \qquad 8 \\ \hline \end{array}$$

13
$$\begin{array}{r} 135,211 \\ \times \qquad 6 \\ \hline \end{array}$$

Solve. Watch the signs.

14
$$\begin{array}{r} 35 \\ \times \ 35 \\ \hline \end{array}$$

15
$$\begin{array}{r} 64 \\ + \ 97 \\ \hline \end{array}$$

16
$$\begin{array}{r} 6043 \\ - \ 718 \\ \hline \end{array}$$

17
$$\begin{array}{r} 4145 \\ - \ 567 \\ \hline \end{array}$$

18
$$\begin{array}{r} 60 \\ \times \ 50 \\ \hline \end{array}$$

19
$$\begin{array}{r} 3723 \\ + \ 685 \\ \hline \end{array}$$

20
$$\begin{array}{r} 2805 \\ + \ 495 \\ \hline \end{array}$$

21
$$\begin{array}{r} 64 \\ - \ 25 \\ \hline \end{array}$$

22
$$\begin{array}{r} 608 \\ \times \ 75 \\ \hline \end{array}$$

23
$$\begin{array}{r} 132 \\ \times \ 46 \\ \hline \end{array}$$

Solve these problems.

A pound of apples costs 98¢. Jo uses 4 pounds to make an apple pie.

24 What is the cost in cents for enough apples to make one apple pie? _____

25 What is the cost in dollars for one apple pie? _____

Name_____

Divide. Watch for remainders.

1 2)96

2 4)288

3 5)645

4 8)728

5 3)244

6 4)512

7 9)189

8 6)936

9 7)0

10 8)92

11 9)503

12 5)722

13 9)112

14 2)639

15 4)712

16 7)216

17 5)55

18 5)555

19 5)556

20 5)557

21 2)200

22 4)200

23 8)200

24 8)207

25 3)75

26 3)437

27 7)285

28 6)756

29 7)712

30 8)664

31 9)333

32 5)248

33 2)78

34 7)420

35 4)171

Divide.

1 2)468

2 3)7241

3 5)8945

4 7)80,341

5 4)6139

6 3)90,124

7 8)11,428

8 9)927

9 6)82,139

10 5)45,560

11 8)2032

12 9)5454

 **Solve these problems.**

13 Eight children want to divide $1376 equally. How much should each child get? Will any money be left over? _____

14 Three people want to divide $4457 equally. How much should each person get? How many dollars will be left over? _____

Find the missing digit.

1
$$
\begin{array}{r}
968\ R3 \\
4\overline{)3\square75} \\
\underline{36} \\
27 \\
\underline{24} \\
35 \\
\underline{32} \\
3
\end{array}
$$

□ is ____.

2
$$
\begin{array}{r}
662 \\
\square\overline{)4634} \\
\underline{42} \\
43 \\
\underline{42} \\
14 \\
\underline{14}
\end{array}
$$

□ is ____.

3
$$
\begin{array}{r}
8\square93 \\
9\overline{)74,637} \\
\underline{72} \\
26 \\
\underline{18} \\
83 \\
\underline{81} \\
27 \\
\underline{27}
\end{array}
$$

□ is ____.

4
$$
\begin{array}{r}
985\ R2 \\
3\overline{)2\square57} \\
\underline{27} \\
25 \\
\underline{24} \\
17 \\
\underline{15} \\
2
\end{array}
$$

□ is ____.

5
$$
\begin{array}{r}
4\,553 \\
8\overline{)36,429} \\
\underline{32} \\
44 \\
\underline{40} \\
42 \\
\underline{40} \\
29 \\
\underline{24} \\
\square
\end{array}
$$

□ is ____.

6
$$
\begin{array}{r}
9\,053\ R3 \\
6\overline{)54,\square21} \\
\underline{54} \\
32 \\
\underline{30} \\
21 \\
\underline{18} \\
3
\end{array}
$$

□ is ____.

7
$$
\begin{array}{r}
893\ R2 \\
5\overline{)\square467} \\
\underline{40} \\
46 \\
\underline{45} \\
17 \\
\underline{15} \\
2
\end{array}
$$

□ is ____.

8
$$
\begin{array}{r}
2\,534 \\
\square\overline{)17,738} \\
\underline{14} \\
37 \\
\underline{35} \\
23 \\
\underline{21} \\
28 \\
\underline{28}
\end{array}
$$

□ is ____.

Name_____

Find the missing digit.

1 $8\overline{)418}$ 52 R □
$$\underline{40}$$
18
$$\underline{16}$$
2

□ is ____.

2 $6\overline{)540}$ 90
$$\underline{□4}$$

□ is ____.

3 $2\overline{)17□}$ 8 9 R1
$$\underline{16}$$
19
$$\underline{18}$$
1

□ is ____.

4 $7\overline{)339}$ 48 R3
$$\underline{□8}$$
59
$$\underline{56}$$
3

□ is ____.

5 $3\overline{)914}$ 3□4 R2
$$\underline{9}$$
14
$$\underline{12}$$
2

□ is ____.

6 $5\overline{)504}$ 100 R4
$$\underline{5}$$
□

□ is ____.

7 $9\overline{)175}$ 19 R□
$$\underline{9}$$
85
$$\underline{81}$$
4

□ is ____.

8 $6\overline{)161}$ □6 R5
$$\underline{12}$$
41
$$\underline{36}$$
5

□ is ____.

9 $3\overline{)268}$ □9 R1
$$\underline{24}$$
28
$$\underline{27}$$
1

□ is ____.

10 $4\overline{)540}$ 1 3 5
$$\underline{4}$$
14
$$\underline{1□}$$
20
$$\underline{20}$$

□ is ____.

11 $8\overline{)366}$ □5 R6
$$\underline{32}$$
46
$$\underline{40}$$
6

□ is ____.

12 $6\overline{)□20}$ 1 0 3 R2
$$\underline{6}$$
20
$$\underline{18}$$
2

□ is ____.

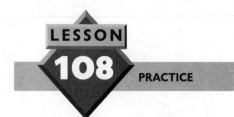
Name_____

Solve these problems.

Tim wants to buy some popcorn. An 8-ounce bag costs $1.60.
A 12-ounce bag costs $1.80.

1 How much does the popcorn cost per ounce in the 8-ounce bag?   _____

2 How much does the popcorn cost per ounce in the 12-ounce bag?   _____

3 Which is the better buy?   _____

Carol wants to buy some peanuts. She can buy a 3-pound bag for
$2.55 or a 5-pound bag for $4.40.

4 How much do the peanuts cost per pound in the 5-pound bag?   _____

5 How much do the peanuts cost per pound in the 3-pound bag?   _____

6 Which is the better buy?   _____

7 Eight erasers cost $1.28. How much is that per eraser?   _____

8 Five bananas cost $1.10. How much is that per banana?   _____

9 Six containers of yogurt cost $4.14. How much is that per
container?   _____

10 A box of 12 cookies costs $1.08. How much is that per cookie?   _____

11 Three tubes of toothpaste cost $6.87. How much is that per
tube?   _____

12 Eight tangerines cost $2.80. How much is that per tangerine?   _____

13 A four-bottle package of juice costs $1.16. How much is that
per bottle?   _____

14 An 8-ounce package of cheese costs $2.00. A 16-ounce
package of cheese costs $3.36. Which is the better buy?   _____

Divide. Check your answers to the first five problems by multiplying.

1 8)232   Check: Does 8 × _____ = 232?

2 5)750   Check: Does 5 × _____ = 750?

3 3)953   Check: Does 3 × _____ + _____ = 953?

4 7)604   Check: Does 7 × _____ + _____ = 604?

5 2)857   Check: Does 2 × _____ + _____ = 857?

Divide. Use shortcuts when you can.

6 4)716   **7** 9)515   **8** 6)139   **9** 3)583   **10** 5)394

11 2)1686   **12** 1)13,945   **13** 4)64   **14** 7)58   **15** 5)922

16 5)200   **17** 4)528   **18** 7)119   **19** 8)405   **20** 3)16

21 3)12   **22** 6)328   **23** 2)19   **24** 9)66   **25** 1)16,452

Here are 12 division problems worked out. There are six incorrect answers. Write *correct* or *incorrect* for each problem.

① 4)2040 — 580

② 5)825 — 165

③ 9)936 — 104

④ 8)504 — 63

_____ _____ _____ _____

⑤ 6)1236 — 260

⑥ 3)759 — 213

⑦ 2)398 — 199

⑧ 7)735 — 150

_____ _____ _____ _____

⑨ 8)1608 — 210

⑩ 4)660 — 165

⑪ 6)762 — 127

⑫ 3)261 — 97

_____ _____ _____ _____

Solve these problems.

⑬ Nine people decided to share $1620 equally. They approximated how much each person should get. Write *yes* or *no* to show if their approximations are reasonable.

   a. Larry thought each person ought to get about $18. _____

   b. Marge thought she should get about $180. _____

   c. Cassandra thought each person should get about $1800. _____

⑭ Four people decide to share $1000 equally. How much should each person get? _____

⑮ Seven people decide to share $763 equally. How much should each person get? _____

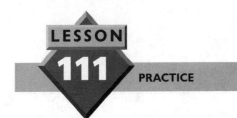

LESSON
111
PRACTICE

Name_____

Solve these problems.

Mrs. George needs 32 muffins for a class picnic. Muffins come in packages of six.

1 How many packages should she buy? _____

2 How many extra muffins will she have? _____

Mr. Brown bought six pencils for $1.32.

3 How much did each pencil cost? _____

4 How much would 25 pencils cost? _____

Tracy baked 40 cookies. She wants to divide the cookies equally among nine children.

5 How many cookies should she give each child? _____

6 Will there be any cookies left over? If so, how many? _____

There are 235 students going on a field trip. Each van can take seven students.

7 How many vans will be needed to take the students on their field trip? _____

Divide. Use shortcuts when you can.

8 $4\overline{)362}$ **9** $5\overline{)123}$ **10** $9\overline{)540}$ **11** $3\overline{)641}$ **12** $5\overline{)302}$

13 $3\overline{)563}$ **14** $8\overline{)124}$ **15** $7\overline{)249}$ **16** $4\overline{)404}$ **17** $9\overline{)63}$

Name_____

Find the average of each set of numbers. Use shortcuts when you can.

1 4, 5, 6, 7, 8 _____

2 19, 20, 21, 22, 23 _____

3 15, 20, 25, 30, 35 _____

4 12, 15, 21, 19, 10, 7 _____

5 66, 66, 66, 66, 66, 66, 66 _____

6 1, 2, 3, 4, 5, 6, 7, 8, 9, 5 _____

7 42, 61, 88, 24, 35 _____

8 4634, 4635, 4636, 4637, 4638 _____

9 37, 47, 57, 67, 77, 87 _____

10 25, 49, 73, 37, 61 _____

11 340, 360, 400, 380, 420 _____

12 3912, 3914, 3918, 3920, 3922, 3916 _____

Solve these problems.

13 Rita bowled three games. Her scores were 182, 173, and 209.

   a. What was her average score for the three games? _____

   b. If Rita bowled a fourth game and scored 188, what would her average score be for the four games? _____

14 Molly took four math tests. Her grades were 95, 83, 74, and 88.

   a. What was her average grade for the four tests? _____

   b. If Molly took a fifth test and received a grade of 85, what would her average grade for the five tests be? _____

Name_____

For each of the following sets of numbers, find the mean, the median, and the mode.

1 10, 3, 17, 8, 12, 3, 9, 4 _____

2 14, 10, 10, 11, 12, 11, 12, 12, 14, 13, 14, 13, 13, 12 _____

3 83, 54, 72, 64, 90, 56, 83 _____

4 9, 8, 3, 0, 8, 4, 10, 7, 5, 4, 8, 2 _____

The heights of 14 students, in centimeters, was recorded. The heights are:
121, 120, 121, 126, 130, 134, 160, 147, 142, 152, 150, 128, 140, 124

5 What is the average height of the students? _____

6 What is the median height of the students? _____

7 What is the mode of the heights of the students? _____

Two math classes took the same test. The scores are as follows:
Class 1: 93, 93, 76, 93, 87, 86, 86, 81, 86, 80, 80, 79, 76, 75, 72, 62, 60, 60, 57, 58
Class 2: 95, 92, 92, 92, 66, 67, 75, 68, 77, 77, 82, 79, 84, 83, 87, 87, 90, 85, 85, 90

8 What is the mean of the scores for Class 1? _____

9 What is the median of the scores for Class 1? _____

10 What is the mode of the scores for Class 1? _____

11 What is the mean of the scores for Class 2? _____

12 What is the median of the scores for Class 2? _____

13 What is the mode of the scores for Class 2? _____

14 Which class did better on the test? Explain your answer.

_____

Divide. Look for patterns that will help you find answers quickly.

1 4)‾20‾

2 4)‾200‾

3 4)‾2000‾

4 4)‾20,000‾

5 5)‾200‾

6 6)‾200‾

7 7)‾200‾

8 8)‾200‾

9 2)‾148‾

10 3)‾384‾

11 4)‾1636‾

12 5)‾926‾

Divide to solve for _n_.

13 $700 \div 7 = n$

n = _____

14 $360 \div 3 = n$

n = _____

15 $48 \div 6 = n$

n = _____

16 $3753 \div 9 = n$

n = _____

17 $420 \div 7 = n$

n = _____

18 $420 \div 3 = n$

n = _____

19 $420 \div 5 = n$

n = _____

20 $1398 \div 6 = n$

n = _____

Solve these problems.

Sam wants to give a whistle to each of the 17 people coming to his birthday party. The whistles come in packages of six.

21 How many packages does he need to buy? _____

22 How many extra whistles will he have? _____

Mrs. Simms cut a pan of brownies into 24 servings. She wishes to serve nine friends.

23 How many brownies should she serve each friend? _____

24 How many brownies will be left over? _____

114 • *Math Explorations and Applications* Level 4

Remember: 8 fluid ounces = 1 cup; 2 cups = 1 pint;
8 pints = 1 gallon; 4 quarts = 1 gallon.

1 How many gallons are there in 64 pints? _____

2 How many cups are there in 64 fluid ounces? _____

3 How many fluid ounces are there in 10 cups? _____

4 How many pints are there in 5 gallons? _____

Remember: 1000 milliliters = 1 liter.

5 How many milliliters are there in 7 liters? _____

6 How many liters are there in 10,000 milliliters? _____

Solve. Watch the signs.

7	**8**	**9**	**10**	**11**
205 $\times$ 125	642 $+$ 978	5183 $-$ 625	10,000 $-$ 5267	300 $\times$ 50

12	**13**	**14**	**15**	**16**
1823 $+$ 6389	650 $+$ 450	1000 $-$ 489	80 $\times$ 70	703 $\times$ 319

Solve for *n*.

17 $8 \times 6 = n$ $n =$ _____

18 $0 \div 5 = n$ $n =$ _____

19 $n = 24 - 6$ $n =$ _____

20 $n = 6 \times 4$ $n =$ _____

21 $38 \times 12 = n$ $n =$ _____

22 $3 \times 0 = n$ $n =$ _____

23 $n = 588 \div 7$ $n =$ _____

24 $500 - 234 = n$ $n =$ _____

25 $n = 336 + 164$ $n =$ _____

26 $381 \div 3 = n$ $n =$ _____

For each of the following rules find four ordered pairs of numbers. On a separate sheet of paper, graph the ordered pairs. Try to draw a line through the four points.

1 The first number is the length in inches of the short side of a rectangle whose long side is four times as long. The second number is the perimeter in inches of the rectangle.

_____

2 The first number is the length in inches of the short side of a rectangle whose long side is four times as long. The second number is the area in square inches of the rectangle.

_____

Find the missing digit.

3
```
      142
   6)□52
      6
      25
      24
      12
      12
```
□ is ____.

4
```
      236 R2
   4)946
      □
      14
      12
      26
      24
       2
```
□ is ____.

5
```
      3□7
   3)951
      9
      5
      3
      21
```
□ is ____.

6
```
      6□ R4
   5)344
      30
      44
      40
       4
```
□ is ____.

7
```
      10□ R2
   8)842
      8
      42
      40
       2
```
□ is ____.

8
```
      239
   □)717
      6
      11
       9
      27
      27
```
□ is ____.

9
```
      1□9 R1
   7)904
      7
      20
      14
      64
      63
       1
```
□ is ____.

10
```
      □6 R3
   9)687
      63
      57
      54
       3
```
□ is ____.

Name_____

Use the graph to approximate how much each of these items costs in dollars.

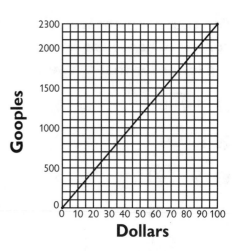

Goonles

Dollars

① Radio—2000 gooples _____   **②** Lamp—820 gooples _____

③ Sunglasses—432 gooples _____   **④** Book—98 gooples _____

⑤ Clock—1220 gooples _____   **⑥** Tennis shoes—1760 gooples _____

In each problem find the value of *x* or *y*. The answers to the problems on the left will help you solve the problems on the right.

❼ 7 —(×245)→ *y* _____   **❽** *x* ←(÷245)— 1715 _____

❾ 46 —(×12)→ *y* _____   **❿** *x* ←(÷12)— 552 _____

⓫ 87 —(×10)→ *y* _____   **⓬** *x* ←(÷10)— 870 _____

⓭ 19 —(×81)→ *y* _____   **⓮** *x* ←(÷81)— 1539 _____

⓯ 30 —(×65)→ *y* _____   **⓰** *x* ←(÷65)— 1950 _____

⓱ 52 —(×31)→ *y* _____   **⓲** *x* ←(÷31)— 1612 _____

⓳ 4 —(×63)→ *y* _____   **⓴** *x* ←(÷63)— 252 _____

For each problem several answers are given, but only one is correct. Choose the correct answer without dividing. Then ring the letter for that answer.

1 $11\overline{)88}$ **a.** 6   **b.** 7   **c.** 9   **d.** 10   **e.** 8

2 $10\overline{)120}$ **a.** 8   **b.** 12   **c.** 10   **d.** 14   **e.** 4

3 $50\overline{)500}$ **a.** 5   **b.** 10   **c.** 15   **d.** 20   **e.** 25

4 $25\overline{)625}$ **a.** 15   **b.** 35   **c.** 75   **d.** 100   **e.** 25

5 $12\overline{)360}$ **a.** 30   **b.** 50   **c.** 70   **d.** 90   **e.** 110

6 $12\overline{)84}$ **a.** 7   **b.** 8   **c.** 9   **d.** 10   **e.** 11

7 $14\overline{)196}$ **a.** 12   **b.** 16   **c.** 14   **d.** 20   **e.** 18

8 $15\overline{)180}$ **a.** 9   **b.** 11   **c.** 15   **d.** 14   **e.** 12

9 $18\overline{)198}$ **a.** 11   **b.** 14   **c.** 17   **d.** 20   **e.** 23

10 $30\overline{)3000}$ **a.** 50   **b.** 75   **c.** 100   **d.** 150   **e.** 200

11 $21\overline{)63}$ **a.** 2   **b.** 3   **c.** 4   **d.** 5   **e.** 6

12 $30\overline{)120}$ **a.** 1   **b.** 2   **c.** 3   **d.** 4   **e.** 5

13 $13\overline{)182}$ **a.** 11   **b.** 14   **c.** 17   **d.** 19   **e.** 24

14 $19\overline{)209}$ **a.** 7   **b.** 9   **c.** 11   **d.** 13   **e.** 15

15 $12\overline{)180}$ **a.** 15   **b.** 18   **c.** 20   **d.** 22   **e.** 25

16 $25\overline{)200}$ **a.** 4   **b.** 5   **c.** 6   **d.** 7   **e.** 8

17 $70\overline{)630}$ **a.** 6   **b.** 7   **c.** 8   **d.** 9   **e.** 10

18 $12\overline{)144}$ **a.** 10   **b.** 12   **c.** 14   **d.** 16   **e.** 18

19 $11\overline{)121}$ **a.** 7   **b.** 9   **c.** 11   **d.** 13   **e.** 15

20 $90\overline{)360}$ **a.** 12   **b.** 10   **c.** 8   **d.** 6   **e.** 4

Name_____

Write the factors of each of the following numbers.

1 24 _____

2 10 _____

3 12 _____

4 7 _____

5 32 _____

6 23 _____

7 8 _____

8 15 _____

9 20 _____

10 19 _____

How many factors does each of the following numbers have?

11 13 _____

12 18 _____

13 21 _____

14 9 _____

15 11 _____

16 16 _____

17 5 _____

18 22 _____

19 25 _____

20 30 _____

Answer these questions. Remember: Prime numbers have exactly two factors. Composite numbers have more than two factors.

21 List three prime numbers. _____

22 List three composite numbers. _____

Determine whether the following numbers are prime or composite.

23 42 _____

24 19 _____

25 14 _____

26 27 _____

27 29 _____

28 28 _____

29 46 _____

30 50 _____

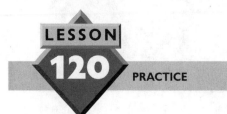

Name_____

Northridge School is raising money for a new movie projector by
selling pizzas. This bar graph shows how many pizzas each class has
sold so far.

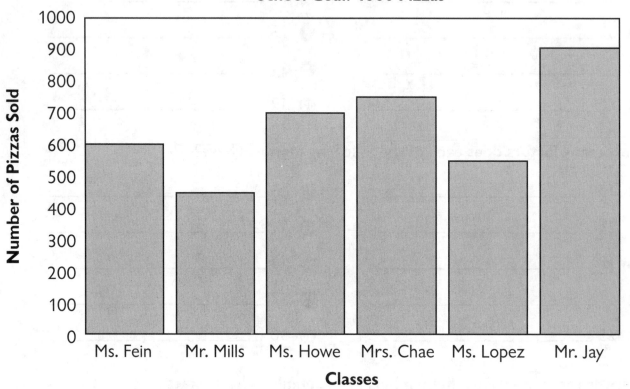

School Goal: 4000 Pizzas

Use the graph to answer these questions.

❶ How many pizzas has Mrs. Chae's class sold?   _____

❷ Which class has sold the most pizzas so far?   _____

❸ How many pizzas has that class sold?   _____

❹ Which class has sold the fewest pizzas so far?   _____

❺ How many pizzas has that class sold?   _____

❻ How many pizzas have been sold all together?   _____

❼ How many more pizzas must be sold for the school to meet
its goal?   _____

The following is Mr. Brooks's December telephone bill.

The Marketville Telephone Company			John Brooks
Monthly Statement			712 East 14th St.
December			Marketville
		Telephone Number	555-6521

Date	Calls to	Number of Minutes	Cost
Dec. 3	Orange Town	6	$1.80
Dec. 8	Raspberry River	12	$2.40
Dec. 11	Lemon Lake	3	$1.50
Dec. 15	Apple City	5	$3.75
Dec. 25	Mangoville	10	$6.00
Dec. 25	Raspberry River	17	$6.80
Dec. 30	Raspberry River	8	$1.60

All calls to other cities are charged by the minute.
The farther a city is from Marketville, the higher the rate.

Answer these questions.

How much does it cost per minute to call each of the following places?

1 Orange Town _____

2 Raspberry River _____

3 Lemon Lake _____

4 Apple City _____

5 Mangoville _____

6 Which city is farther from Marketville—Mangoville or Lemon Lake? _____

7 There is an error in one of the charges on Mr. Brooks's bill. How much will Mr. Brooks save if he finds the error? _____

8 Order the cities Mr. Brooks called, from farthest from to nearest to Marketville.

_____

9 For how many minutes did Mr. Brooks use the telephone in December on calls to other cities? _____

10 After the error was corrected, what was the total cost of Mr. Brooks's December telephone bill? _____

Name_____

Solve these problems.

1 Vanessa bought seven cans of fruit. She was charged $2.73. How much did each can of fruit cost? _____

2 Jorge's family has six people. They want to share four large pizzas equally. Each large pizza is cut into 12 slices. How many slices will each family member get? _____

3 Mrs. Scott drove 455 kilometers in seven hours. What was her average speed? _____

4 Mr. Thomas drove 265 kilometers in four hours. About what was his average speed? _____

5 Will can buy eight doughnuts for $1.28. What is the cost per doughnut? _____

6 Kim bought five apples that cost 26¢ each. The tax was 17¢. She paid with a $5 bill. How much change should she get back? _____

7 The fourth-grade class needed to raise $1800 for a class trip. The students earned $420 from a popcorn sale and $750 from a fruit sale. How much did they still need? _____

8 Mark ran every day for seven days. He ran the following distances on those days: 12 kilometers, 15 kilometers, 8 kilometers, 14 kilometers, 6 kilometers, 12 kilometers, 10 kilometers. What is the average distance Mark ran each day? _____

For each problem several answers are given, but only one is correct. Choose the correct answer without dividing.

9 $17\overline{)102}$ **a.** 3   **b.** 4   **c.** 5   **d.** 6   **e.** 7

10 $100\overline{)740,000}$ **a.** 740   **b.** 148   **c.** 7400   **d.** 1480   **e.** 74

11 $9\overline{)85}$ **a.** 9 R5   **b.** 9 R3   **c.** 9 R4   **d.** 8 R5   **e.** 8 R6

Name_____

Solve for *n*. Watch the signs.

1 $n + 35 = 53$

$n =$ _____

2 $9 \times 8 = n$

$n =$ _____

3 $63 \div n = 9$

$n =$ _____

4 $n = 56 \div 7$

$n =$ _____

5 $32 - n = 29$

$n =$ _____

6 $n \div 3 = 8$

$n =$ _____

7 $n = 7 \times 5$

$n =$ _____

8 $36 - 28 = n$

$n =$ _____

9 $n = 6 \times 4$

$n =$ _____

10 $n + 17 = 46$

$n =$ _____

11 $n = 17 + 8$

$n =$ _____

12 $42 \div 6 = n$

$n =$ _____

Multiply.

13 $100 \times 20 =$ _____

14 $43 \times 10 =$ _____

15 $10,000 \times 56 =$ _____

16 $1000 \times 56 =$ _____

17 $30 \times 101 =$ _____

18 $300 \times 101 =$ _____

Solve. Watch the signs. Use shortcuts when you can.

19 $7 \times 4 =$ _____

20 $80 \div 4 =$ _____

21 $62 + 19 =$ _____

22 $11 \times 14 =$ _____

23 $42 - 15 =$ _____

24 $56 \div 7 =$ _____

25 $46 - 38 =$ _____

26 $38 \div 2 =$ _____

27 $22 + 49 =$ _____

Divide. Use shortcuts when you can.

28 $6 \overline{)636}$

29 $8 \overline{)8000}$

30 $5 \overline{)350}$

31 $4 \overline{)200}$

32 $4 \overline{)400}$

33 $8 \overline{)400}$

34 $4 \overline{)800}$

35 $2 \overline{)4008}$

Name_____

Divide. Watch for remainders.

1 $4\overline{)75}$ **2** $6\overline{)2088}$ **3** $8\overline{)125}$ **4** $9\overline{)1809}$ **5** $6\overline{)1000}$

6 $3\overline{)6147}$ **7** $8\overline{)20,000}$ **8** $4\overline{)603}$ **9** $7\overline{)441}$ **10** $5\overline{)910}$

Solve for *n*. Watch the signs.

11 $n = 360 \div 4$ $n =$ _____ **12** $n + 23 = 52$ $n =$ _____ **13** $n = 12 \times 8$ $n =$ _____

14 $8 + 13 = n$ $n =$ _____ **15** $n = 20 \times 6$ $n =$ _____ **16** $16 + n = 23$ $n =$ _____

Find the mean, median, and mode of each set of numbers.

17 14, 9, 2, 7, 9, 13   _____

18 140, 90, 20, 70, 90, 130   _____

Solve these problems.

19 Marchita has $5. Does she have enough money to buy 12 cookies at 32¢ each?   _____

20 Karen can buy six bags of popcorn for $4.50. How much does each bag of popcorn cost?   _____

21 Ken baby-sits after school each day. He earned $6 on Monday, $8 on Tuesday, $8 on Wednesday, $12 on Thursday, and $4 on Friday. What is the average amount he earned per day?   _____

22 Nancy drinks four glasses of milk a day. How many glasses of milk does she drink in a week?   _____

23 Alonzo drove 342 kilometers in six hours. What was his average speed?   _____

Name_____

Divide.

1 $6)\overline{58}$ **2** $3)\overline{87}$ **3** $4)\overline{320}$ **4** $5)\overline{613}$ **5** $7)\overline{1123}$

6 $4)\overline{836}$ **7** $7)\overline{3225}$ **8** $2)\overline{504}$ **9** $8)\overline{1009}$ **10** $3)\overline{400}$

Solve for n. Watch the signs.

11 $n = 14 \times 23$ $n =$ _____ **12** $n + 13 = 41$ $n =$ _____ **13** $20 \times n = 800$ $n =$ _____

14 $56 - n = 39$ $n =$ _____ **15** $n = 42 \div 7$ $n =$ _____ **16** $n - 16 = 32$ $n =$ _____

17 $n \div 7 = 9$ $n =$ _____ **18** $n = 36 \times 12$ $n =$ _____ **19** $n + 14 = 70$ $n =$ _____

Find the mean, median, and mode for each set of numbers.

20 3, 8, 9, 7, 8 _____ **21** 2, 4, 6, 8, 10 _____

22 63, 88, 92, 80, 77 _____ **23** 14, 8, 9, 8, 11 _____

Solve these problems.

24 Dan needs 32 favors for his party. The favors come in packages of six. How many packages will he need? _____

25 Terry bought a can of soup for 43¢ and a bagel for 29¢. She was charged 76¢ for the two items, including tax. How much was the tax? _____

26 Ricardo got these scores on three English tests: 76, 82, 70. What was his average score for the three tests? _____

Name_____

What fraction of each of the following figures has been shaded?

1  _____

2 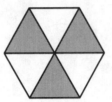 _____

3 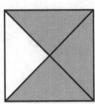 _____

4  _____

5 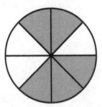 _____

6 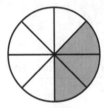 _____

7 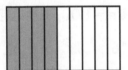 _____

8 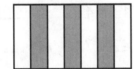 _____

9 _____

What fraction of each of the following sets has a ring around it?

10 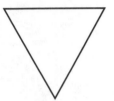 _____

11  _____

12 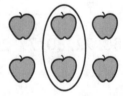 _____

13 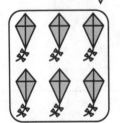 _____

14  _____

15  _____

16  _____

17 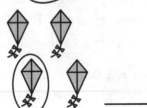 _____

18  _____

Name_____

Solve.

1 $\dfrac{1}{3}$ of 24 = _____

2 $\dfrac{1}{2}$ of 24 = _____

3 $\dfrac{3}{4}$ of 24 = _____

4 $\dfrac{5}{6}$ of 24 = _____

5 $\dfrac{1}{6}$ of 18 = _____

6 $\dfrac{2}{3}$ of 18 = _____

7 $\dfrac{1}{4}$ of 60 = _____

8 $\dfrac{3}{10}$ of 60 = _____

9 $\dfrac{1}{3}$ of 60 = _____

10 $\dfrac{1}{9}$ of 36 = _____

11 $\dfrac{2}{9}$ of 36 = _____

12 $\dfrac{3}{8}$ of 16 = _____

13 $\dfrac{1}{4}$ of 16 = _____

14 $\dfrac{1}{5}$ of 30 = _____

15 $\dfrac{2}{3}$ of 30 = _____

Solve these problems.

16 A coat that sells for $48 is on sale for $\frac{1}{4}$ off.

a. How much is $\frac{1}{4}$ of 48? _____

b. What is the sale price of the coat? _____

Remember: 8 ounces = 1 cup.

17 A 4-cup container of milk is $\frac{1}{8}$ full. How many ounces are in the container? _____

18 Sally is typing her English paper. Her paper is 200 words long. She has typed 80 words so far. Has she typed more than $\frac{3}{8}$ of the paper? _____

19 Mrs. King's fourth-grade class has 30 students. Girls make up $\frac{2}{5}$ of the students. How many girls are in Mrs. King's fourth-grade class? _____

Name_____

Answer these questions.

A probability is a number that tells what fraction of the time
something is expected to happen.

1 If you roll a cube numbered 0–5, what do you think is the
probability that the number showing will be a 4?   _____

2 If you roll a cube numbered 0–5, what do you think is the
probability that the number showing will be a 0?   _____

3 If you roll a cube numbered 0–5, what do you think is the
probability that the number showing will be even?   _____

4 If you roll a cube numbered 0–5, what do you think is the
probability that the number showing will be less than 3?   _____

5 If you roll a cube numbered 0–5, what do you think is the
probability that the number showing will be greater than 2?   _____

6 If you roll a cube numbered 0–5, what do you think is the
probability that the number showing will be less than 6?   _____

Suppose you have a jar of 100 jelly beans. Of those, 30 are red,
45 are green, 15 are white, and 10 are yellow.

7 If you take a jelly bean from the jar without looking, what do you
think is the probability that the jelly bean you choose will be green?   _____

8 If you take a jelly bean from the jar without looking, what do you
think is the probability that the jelly bean you choose will be white?   _____

9 If you take a jelly bean from the jar without looking, what do you
think is the probability that the jelly bean you choose will be orange?   _____

10 If you take a jelly bean from the jar without looking, what do you
think is the probability that the jelly bean you choose will be red
or yellow?   _____

Max and Tess are spinning a spinner that has the colors red, white, yellow, blue, green, and black. Max wins if the color red or green is spun. Tess wins if white, yellow, blue, or green is spun.

1 Who do you think will win more often?   _____

2 What fraction of the time do you think Tess will win?   _____

3 If they spin the spinner 6 times, how many times would you expect Tess to win?   _____

4 What is $\frac{4}{6}$ of 6?   _____

5 Tess's probability of winning is $\frac{4}{6}$. What is Max's probability of winning?   _____

Here is an experiment Tess did with her class. Each student spun the 6 colored spinners 6 times. Each student kept track of how many times he or she spun the color blue in the 6 spins. Tess made a chart to show how many of the students did not spin blue at all, how many spun blue one time, and so on.

Number of Times Blue Was Spun in 6 Tries	Number of Students
0	8
1	11
2	3
3	2
4	1
5	0
6	0

6 How many students took part in Tess's experiment?   _____

7 How many students in the class spun blue
   a. 1 out of 6 times?   **b.** 2 out of 6 times?   **c.** 3 out of 6 times?

   _____   _____   _____

   d. 4 out of 6 times?   **e.** 5 out of 6 times?   **f.** 6 out of 6 times?

   _____   _____   _____

   g. 0 out of 6 times?

   _____

Name_____

Solve these problems.

1 If $\frac{3}{4}$ of the 24 students in Susan's class are right-handed, how many students are left-handed? _____

2 Luis can save $\frac{1}{3}$ the cost of a baseball glove if he waits for a sale. The glove costs $27.00. How much will Luis save if he waits for the sale? _____

3 If $\frac{2}{5}$ of Mr. Fishman's students are girls, and he has 30 students in his class, how many of his students are boys? _____

Write the correct amount.

4 $\frac{1}{4}$ of 20 = _____   **5** $\frac{3}{5}$ of 25 = _____   **6** $\frac{2}{7}$ of 14 = _____

7 $\frac{2}{5}$ of 40 = _____   **8** $\frac{5}{6}$ of 36 = _____   **9** $\frac{2}{3}$ of 48 = _____

10 $\frac{1}{6}$ of 60 = _____   **11** $\frac{5}{10}$ of 100 = _____   **12** $\frac{3}{4}$ of 44 = _____

13 $\frac{3}{4}$ of 72 = _____   **14** $\frac{3}{3}$ of 10 = _____   **15** $\frac{5}{6}$ of 60 = _____

16 $\frac{2}{3}$ of 45 = _____   **17** $\frac{2}{4}$ of 30 = _____   **18** $\frac{1}{8}$ of 88 = _____

19 $\frac{4}{5}$ of 80 = _____   **20** $\frac{2}{6}$ of 54 = _____   **21** $\frac{3}{5}$ of 70 = _____

22 $\frac{1}{7}$ of 49 = _____   **23** $\frac{1}{5}$ of 15 = _____   **24** $\frac{4}{9}$ of 27 = _____

25 $\frac{1}{2}$ of 100 = _____   **26** $\frac{1}{4}$ of 16 = _____   **27** $\frac{1}{4}$ of 100 = _____

28 $\frac{1}{10}$ of 50 = _____   **29** $\frac{1}{2}$ of 40 = _____   **30** $\frac{2}{4}$ of 90 = _____

Name_____

What fraction of the rectangle is shaded?

1

2

3

_____   _____   _____

What fraction of the circle is shaded?

4

5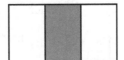

6

7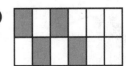

_____   _____   _____   _____

Ring the greater fraction.

8 $\frac{1}{4}$ or $\frac{3}{8}$

9 $\frac{5}{8}$ or $\frac{1}{2}$

10 $\frac{3}{4}$ or $\frac{7}{8}$

 Solve these problems.

Grant and Iris are spinning a spinner that has the colors red, white, yellow, blue, green, and black. Iris wins if the color blue, red, black, or white is spun. Grant wins if yellow or green is spun.

11 What is the probability that Iris will win?   _____

12 What is the probability that Grant will win?   _____

Name_____

What fraction of each figure is shaded?

1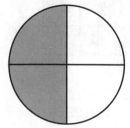

2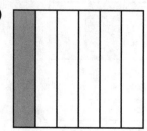

3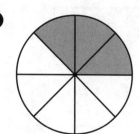

_____   _____   _____

Draw <, >, or = to make each statement true.

4 $\frac{3}{5}$ ◯ $\frac{4}{5}$ **5** $\frac{2}{4}$ ◯ $\frac{1}{2}$ **6** $\frac{3}{4}$ ◯ $\frac{1}{2}$ **7** $\frac{1}{2}$ ◯ $\frac{1}{3}$ **8** $\frac{2}{5}$ ◯ $\frac{3}{4}$

Convert each fraction to a fraction that is equivalent but has a denominator of 18.

9 $\frac{1}{3} = \frac{\square}{18}$ **10** $\frac{1}{6} = \frac{\square}{18}$ **11** $\frac{1}{2} = \frac{\square}{18}$ **12** $\frac{1}{9} = \frac{\square}{18}$ **13** $\frac{2}{3} = \frac{\square}{18}$ **14** $\frac{4}{9} = \frac{\square}{18}$

Solve these problems.

15 Maxine baked 20 cookies. Rory ate seven cookies. Did Rory eat more or less than $\frac{2}{5}$ of the cookies?   _____

16 Mark earns $9 each week. How much does he earn in one year?   _____

17 A movie lasts 1 hour and 20 minutes. If the movie begins at 3:10 P.M., what time will it end?   _____

18 Samantha typed $\frac{3}{5}$ of a 200-word essay for history. Greg typed $\frac{1}{4}$ of a 300-word essay for history.

    a. Who typed more words?   _____

    b. How many more words?   _____

Write a mixed number to show how many.

1  _____ bars of soap

2 ⬭ ⬭ ⬭ ◔ _____ circles

3 🥧 🥧 🥧 ◖ _____ pies

Change each improper fraction to a mixed number or whole number.

4 $\dfrac{27}{6}$ = _____ **5** $\dfrac{7}{2}$ = _____ **6** $\dfrac{18}{9}$ = _____

7 $\dfrac{8}{3}$ = _____ **8** $\dfrac{7}{4}$ = _____ **9** $\dfrac{13}{6}$ = _____

10 $\dfrac{35}{7}$ = _____ **11** $\dfrac{16}{5}$ = _____ **12** $\dfrac{19}{4}$ = _____

Change each mixed number to an improper fraction.

13 $3\dfrac{1}{5}$ = _____ **14** $9\dfrac{2}{7}$ = _____ **15** $5\dfrac{2}{3}$ = _____

16 $16\dfrac{1}{2}$ = _____ **17** $11\dfrac{3}{4}$ = _____ **18** $6\dfrac{7}{10}$ = _____

19 $1\dfrac{4}{9}$ = _____ **20** $2\dfrac{7}{8}$ = _____ **21** $6\dfrac{1}{3}$ = _____

Name_____

Estimate the length. Then measure to the nearest $\frac{1}{8}$ inch.

1

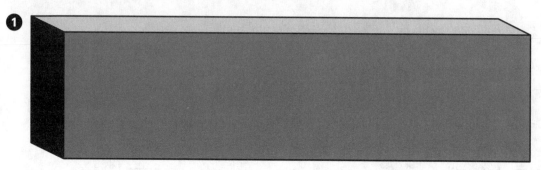

Your estimate _____   Actual measure _____

2

Your estimate _____   Actual measure _____

3

Your estimate _____   Actual measure _____

4

Your estimate _____   Actual measure _____

5

Your estimate _____   Actual measure _____

Name_____

Figure out the answer. Then draw line segments and measure to check.

1 $\frac{3}{4}$ inch + $\frac{1}{8}$ inch = _____

2 $1\frac{1}{4}$ inch + $\frac{1}{2}$ inch = _____

3 $2\frac{1}{2}$ inches − $\frac{1}{4}$ inch = _____

4 $\frac{3}{8}$ inch + $\frac{1}{4}$ inch = _____

5 1 inch − $\frac{1}{4}$ inch = _____

6 $1\frac{3}{8}$ inch + $1\frac{1}{2}$ inch = _____

7 $2\frac{1}{4}$ inches − $\frac{3}{4}$ inch = _____

8 3 inches − $\frac{7}{8}$ inch = _____

Solve these problems.

9 Betsy placed a book that is $\frac{1}{2}$ inch thick on a book that is $\frac{3}{4}$ inch thick. How thick is the stack of two books? _____

10 Corey swam $2\frac{1}{4}$ miles on Saturday and $2\frac{3}{4}$ miles on Sunday. How many miles did he swim in those two days? _____

11 Simona bought $1\frac{1}{2}$ pounds of bananas and $2\frac{1}{4}$ pounds of apples. How many pounds of fruit did she buy all together? _____

12 Mr. Grossman had a 4-foot long piece of wood. He cut off $\frac{1}{2}$ foot. How long was the remaining piece of wood? _____

13 Jenny had five dollars. She spent a quarter on a pencil and two dollars on a notebook. How much did she have left? _____

14 Alex bought $\frac{3}{4}$ of a pound of candy. He ate $\frac{1}{8}$ of a pound of the candy. How much candy does Alex have left? _____

Name_____

Answer these questions.

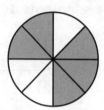

1 What is $\frac{1}{4} + \frac{3}{8}$? _____

2 How many eighths are shaded in the circle all together? _____

3 What is $\frac{1}{2} + \frac{1}{5}$? _____

4 How many tenths are shaded in the circle all together? _____

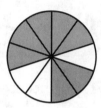

Solve. Watch the signs.

5 $\frac{1}{5} + \frac{2}{5} =$ _____   **6** $\frac{4}{5} - \frac{2}{5} =$ _____   **7** $\frac{1}{2} - \frac{1}{6} =$ _____

8 $\frac{3}{4} - \frac{1}{6} =$ _____   **9** $\frac{1}{2} + \frac{3}{10} =$ _____   **10** $\frac{4}{5} + \frac{1}{10} =$ _____

11 $\frac{7}{8} - \frac{1}{8} =$ _____   **12** $\frac{1}{2} + \frac{3}{8} =$ _____   **13** $\frac{1}{3} + \frac{1}{4} =$ _____

14 $\frac{2}{3} - \frac{7}{12} =$ _____   **15** $\frac{1}{8} + \frac{3}{16} =$ _____   **16** $\frac{11}{16} - \frac{1}{4} =$ _____

17 $\frac{8}{9} - \frac{2}{9} =$ _____   **18** $\frac{3}{7} + \frac{4}{7} =$ _____   **19** $\frac{7}{16} - \frac{3}{8} =$ _____

20 $\frac{1}{3} + \frac{1}{6} =$ _____   **21** $\frac{5}{6} - \frac{1}{6} =$ _____   **22** $\frac{1}{3} + \frac{5}{12} =$ _____

Name_____

Solve. Write your answers as either mixed numbers or proper fractions (or whole numbers if possible).

1 $3\frac{1}{8} + \frac{7}{8} = $ _____

2 $4\frac{5}{32} - 3\frac{1}{8} = $ _____

3 $3 + 1\frac{5}{6} = $ _____

4 $\frac{1}{4} - \frac{1}{8} = $ _____

5 $5\frac{1}{2} - 2\frac{1}{4} = $ _____

6 $5\frac{10}{32} + 1\frac{3}{8} = $ _____

7 $6\frac{3}{4} - 2\frac{6}{8} = $ _____

8 $3\frac{2}{5} + 4\frac{3}{5} = $ _____

9 $5\frac{3}{5} - 2\frac{1}{10} = $ _____

10 $4\frac{2}{3} - 1\frac{1}{8} = $ _____

11 $9\frac{1}{16} + 4\frac{1}{4} = $ _____

12 $\frac{3}{2} + 6\frac{1}{2} = $ _____

13 $4\frac{8}{32} - 2\frac{1}{8} = $ _____

14 $1\frac{5}{16} + 3\frac{3}{8} = $ _____

Solve these problems.

15 Cathy ran $2\frac{1}{2}$ miles on Monday and $3\frac{1}{8}$ miles on Tuesday. How far did she run over the two days? _____

16 Mr. Walters worked $6\frac{1}{4}$ hours on Thursday and $8\frac{3}{4}$ hours on Friday. How many hours did he work over the two days? _____

17 Sam caught a $3\frac{5}{16}$-pound fish. The record for that lake was an $11\frac{1}{2}$-pound fish. How much less did Sam's fish weigh? _____

18 Mia has $1\frac{3}{8}$ cups of flour. She needs $4\frac{3}{4}$ cups of flour for baking. How much more flour does Mia need? _____

Name_____

Write in standard form.

1 2 ones, 3 tenths, 6 hundredths _____

2 4 tens, 0 ones, 0 tenths, 3 hundredths _____

3 4 ones, 2 tenths, 8 hundredths _____

4 2 tens, 2 ones, 4 tenths, 9 hundredths _____

5 2 hundreds, 4 tens, 3 ones, 9 tenths, 2 hundredths _____

6 6 tens, 0 ones, 4 tenths, 5 hundredths _____

7 5 ones, 3 tenths, 7 hundredths _____

8 9 hundreds, 9 tens, 9 ones, 9 tenths _____

9 1 hundred, 0 tens, 1 one, 0 tenths, 1 hundredth _____

10 9 tens, 4 ones, 6 tenths, 3 hundredths _____

11 50 + 8 + 0.6 + 0.05 _____

12 30 + 0 + 0.8 + 0.04 _____

13 90 + 0 + 0.7 + 0.02 _____

14 20 + 1 + 0 + 0.02 _____

15 10 + 9 + 0.6 + 0.08 _____

16 40 + 2 + 0.3 + 0.04 _____

17 60 + 9 + 0.0 + 0.06 _____

Answer these questions.

18 Which is greater, 0.01 or 0.001? _____

19 Which is greater, $\frac{1}{1000}$ or $\frac{1}{10,000}$? _____

20 Which is greater, 000.1 or 0.001? _____

Draw <, >, or = to make each statement true.

1 0.5 ◯ 0.2   **2** 0.6 ◯ 0.8   **3** 0.6 ◯ 0.09   **4** 0.08 ◯ 0.03

5 0.2 ◯ 0.6   **6** 0.09 ◯ 0.1   **7** 0.020 ◯ 0.2   **8** 0.76 ◯ 0.8

9 0.09 ◯ 0.04   **10** 0.6 ◯ 0.06   **11** 0.087 ◯ 0.087   **12** 0.83 ◯ 0.9

13 0.6 ◯ 0.49   **14** 0.408 ◯ 0.532   **15** 0.268 ◯ 0.8   **16** 0.039 ◯ 0.53

Write each amount as a decimal.

17 7 dimes = _____   **18** 23 cents = _____

19 4 dimes and 6 cents = _____   **20** 9 dimes and 0 cents = _____

For each figure show what portion is shaded by writing a fraction and a decimal.

21 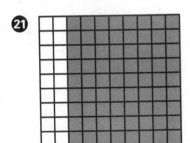   **22** 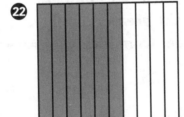   **23**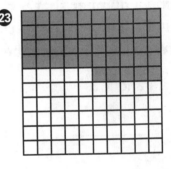

_____   _____   _____

Write each fraction as a decimal.

24 $\dfrac{18}{100}$ = _____   **25** $\dfrac{35}{100}$ = _____   **26** $\dfrac{3428}{10,000}$ = _____

27 $\dfrac{432}{1000}$ = _____   **28** $\dfrac{5}{10}$ = _____   **29** $\dfrac{87}{100}$ = _____

Name_____

Rewrite each set of numbers from least to greatest with a < symbol between each pair to make the statement true.

1 7.8, 8.1, 6.9, 7.79, 8.05, 6.945

_____

2 0.078, 0.081, 0.779, 0.0805, 0.06945, 0.69

_____

3 4.002, 4.03, 3.98, 2.999967, 3, 3.00056

_____

For each of the following pairs of numbers:
a. Find a number that is exactly halfway between.
b. Find a number that is closer to the lesser number.
c. Find a number that is closer to the greater number.
d. Write the three numbers in order from least to greatest.

4 8.4 and 9.3

a. _____ b. _____ c. _____ d. _____

5 7 and 8

a. _____ b. _____ c. _____ d. _____

6 4.003 and 4.004

a. _____ b. _____ c. _____ d. _____

Name_____

Draw <, >, or = to make each statement true.

1 6.8 ◯ 8.6

2 0.91 ◯ 0.893

3 42.6 ◯ 4.26

4 18.31 ◯ 18.310

5 462.5 ◯ 465.2

6 0.834 ◯ 8.1

7 7.76 ◯ 77.6

8 92.3 ◯ 8.14

9 10.62 ◯ 10.0

10 6.4 ◯ 5.9

11 8.3 ◯ 8.300

12 1.037 ◯ 1.03

13 9.11 ◯ 8.10

14 77.36 ◯ 7.367

15 402.0 ◯ 386.9

16 100.0 ◯ 100.001

17 1.5 ◯ 0.92

18 8.8 ◯ 7.31

19 20.003 ◯ 21.0

20 38.090 ◯ 38.09

21 17.282 ◯ 15.91

22 5.6 ◯ 3.8

23 2.0 ◯ 3.14

24 0.7 ◯ 0.05

25 1.09 ◯ 2.0

26 0.518 ◯ 0.518

27 9.091 ◯ 9.087

Which of the following are possible? If possible, draw or write the coins needed. If not possible, tell why.

28 Make 65 cents with eight coins.

_____

29 Make 45 cents with five coins.

_____

30 Make 33 cents with four coins.

_____

Name_____

Round to the nearest hundredth.

1 2.675 _____

2 4.1245 _____

3 0.0016 _____

4 62.3290002 _____

5 6.213 _____

6 4.61739999 _____

7 2.4623001 _____

8 1.817405006 _____

9 5.652 _____

Round to the nearest thousandth.

10 4.315621 _____

11 4.3156 _____

12 2.13590004 _____

13 0.00115 _____

14 6.3078 _____

15 1.90350003 _____

Solve these problems. Round the answers in a way that makes sense.

16 Roman bought a basketball for $16.99. He paid sales tax, which was $1.10435. How much did the basketball cost, including tax? _____

17 Missy is on the diving team. Her scores for a dive are 7.9, 6.9, 7.2, and 7.3. Her average score is 7.325. How should her average score be recorded? _____

18 The fourth-grade classes are going on a field trip. There are 648 people who need to be transported by buses that will carry 52 people each. How many buses are needed for the fourth-grade field trip? _____

19 Sandy has taken six math tests. These are her scores: 75, 86, 91, 78, 87, and 82. She finds her average to be 83.1666667. What score will Sandy get on her report card? _____

Multiply.

1 6.3 × 100 = _____

2 0.41 × 10 = _____

3 42.61 × 100 = _____

4 903.1 × 10 = _____

5 28.418 × 100 = _____

6 10 × 3.034 = _____

7 1000 × 51.073 = _____

8 204.12 × 100 = _____

9 600.3 × 1000 = _____

10 10 × 1.091 = _____

11 0.001 × 1000 = _____

12 10 × 87.32 = _____

13 4.386 × 100 = _____

14 28.26 × 10 = _____

15 100 × 37.3 = _____

16 47.5 × 1000 = _____

17 132.6 × 10 = _____

18 45.32 × 100 = _____

19 10 × 9.5 = _____

20 1000 × 8.76 = _____

Solve. Watch the signs.

21 1000 × 0.54 = _____

22 1000 × 0.867 = _____

23 4.37 × 10 = _____

24 9.7 ÷ 10 = _____

25 6.86 ÷ 100 = _____

26 11.2 ÷ 100 = _____

27 52.5 ÷ 10 = _____

28 100 × 1.45 = _____

29 10 × 11.25 = _____

30 1.234 ÷ 1000 = _____

Solve these problems.

31 How many cents are there in $32.09? _____

32 How many dollars are there in 4360 cents? _____

33 How many meters are there in 1235 centimeters? _____

Multiply or divide. Watch the signs.

1 6.12 ÷ 100 = _____

2 96.8 ÷ 10 = _____

3 3.004 × 1000 = _____

4 96.8 × 100 = _____

5 10 × 91 = _____

6 100 × 7.1 = _____

7 100 × 46.03 = _____

8 3.7 ÷ 10 = _____

9 7.32 ÷ 1000 = _____

10 6321 ÷ 1000 = _____

11 613.1 × 100 = _____

12 43 ÷ 100 = _____

13 54.210 ÷ 10 = _____

14 10 × 7.9 = _____

15 100 × 2.301 = _____

16 83 ÷ 100 = _____

17 60 ÷ 100 = _____

18 0.65 × 1000 = _____

Solve these problems.

19 One month Mrs. Jones made deposits of the following amounts: $346.19, $89.25, and $179.76. She also wrote checks for the following amounts: $20.00, $2.45, $38.23, $171.16, $42.14, $12.39, $9.00, $27.53, and $97.98. Assume Mrs. Jones started with a balance of $250 in her checkbook.

a. What would her balance be at the end of the month? _____

b. What would her balance be if she "rounds off" the amounts each time by dropping the cents? _____

c. What is the difference between the two balances? _____

Find the value of the missing number.

1 6 dm = _____ m

2 4 dm = _____ m

3 7 m = _____ dm

4 _____ dm = 9 m

5 1 m = _____ dm

6 6 m = _____ dm

7 70 m = _____ dm

8 21 cm = _____ m

9 9 cm = _____ m

10 0.42 m = _____ cm

11 _____ cm = 0.09 m

12 _____ cm = 1 m

13 4 mm = _____ m

14 127 mm = _____ m

15 37 mm = _____ m

16 _____ mm = 1 m

17 _____ mm = 0.810 m

18 0.7 m = _____ mm

19 2 km = _____ m

20 12 km = _____ m

21 60 m = _____ km

22 910 m = _____ km

23 1000 m = _____ km

24 3200 m = _____ km

25 9 m = _____ dm

26 850 m = _____ km

27 2300 m = _____ km

28 13 cm = _____ m

29 0.34 m = _____ cm

30 _____ cm = 0.4 m

31 15 km = _____ m

32 11 dm = _____ m

33 18 mm = _____ m

34 0.135 m = _____ mm

35 30 dm = _____ m

36 7 km = _____ m

37 120 cm = _____ m

38 234 mm = _____ m

39 3.40 m = _____ cm

40 3 m = _____ dm

41 1700 m = _____ km

42 0.642 m = _____ mm

43 2000 mm = _____ m

44 _____ dm = 10 m

Name_____

Write the length of each object in millimeters and then in centimeters.

1

Admit One	Theater B showing	Admit One	Theater B showing
	It's a Dog's Life		It's a Dog's Life
	3:30 P.M.		3:30 P.M.

_____   _____

╤╤╤╤╤╤╤╤╤╤╤╤╤╤╤╤╤╤╤╤╤╤╤╤╤╤╤
|1 |2 |3 |4 |5 |6 |7 |8 |9 |10 |11

2

ERASER

_____   _____

╤╤╤╤╤╤╤╤╤╤╤╤╤╤╤╤╤╤╤╤╤╤╤╤╤╤╤
|1 |2 |3 |4 |5 |6 |7 |8 |9 |10 |11

Solve these problems.

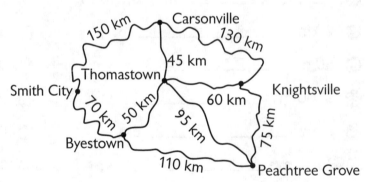

Map labels:
- 150 km — Carsonville
- 130 km
- 45 km
- Thomastown
- Smith City
- Knightsville
- 60 km
- 70 km, 50 km
- 95 km
- 75 km
- Byestown
- 110 km — Peachtree Grove

3 How many kilometers is it from Byestown to Peachtree Grove? _____

4 Which town is closest to Thomastown? _____

5 How many kilometers is it from Carsonville to Peachtree Grove if you go through Thomastown? _____

6 If you were going from Smith City to Thomastown, how much shorter is it to go through Byestown? _____

7 Which town is farthest from Smith City? _____

Name_____

Add or subtract.

① 4.12
   + 3.77

② 1.8
   + 2.72

③ 6.84
   − 2.43

④ 11.64
   + 7.30

⑤ 19.07
   − 2.78

⑥ 9.91
   − 2.38

⑦ 4.03
   − 2.75

⑧ 5.09
   + 4.91

⑨ 2.4
   − 1.27

⑩ 3.9
   − 1.06

⑪ 10.3
   − 2.94

⑫ 4.77
   + 3.53

⑬ 6.07
   − 4.31

⑭ 5.04
   + 3.19

⑮ 7.98
   + 5.02

Add or subtract.

⑯ 1.72 + 3.14 = _____

⑰ 3.5 + 7.5 = _____

⑱ 6.29 − 4.24 = _____

⑲ 8.12 − 4.37 = _____

⑳ 9.65 + 2.7 = _____

㉑ 5.09 + 5.09 = _____

㉒ 3.04 − 2.07 = _____

㉓ 14.72 − 11.1 = _____

Solve these problems.

㉔ Stella swam 200 meters in 1 minute and 49.7 seconds. Janice swam 200 meters in 2 minutes and 3.1 seconds. By how much did Stella beat Janice?

_____

㉕ Roger swam 400 meters in 3 minutes and 47.2 seconds. Was his average speed for his swim more than 2 meters per second?

_____

㉖ Rita swam 100 meters in 52.8 seconds. By how much time did she beat 1 minute?

_____

Solve these problems.

1 A 24-ounce jar of peanut butter costs $3.49. A 16-ounce jar of peanut butter costs $2.69. How much more does the 24-ounce jar cost than the 16-ounce jar? _____

2 Mrs. Green bought a skirt for $24.98 and a blouse for $19.99. How much did Mrs. Green spend all together? _____

3 The Morris family planned to drive 482 kilometers the first day of their vacation. They drove 135.6 kilometers before breakfast and 189.8 kilometers after breakfast. How much farther did they have to drive that day? _____

4 On his first try Bill threw a softball 20.38 meters. On his second try he threw it 24.67 meters. How much farther did Bill throw the softball on the second try? _____

5 Mrs. Simpson has $4136.78 in her checking account. She wrote a check for $23.45 and made a deposit of $135.75. How much is in her checking account now? _____

One box of popcorn costs $2.65.

6 How much will two boxes of popcorn cost? _____

7 How much will four boxes of popcorn cost? _____

8 Before Mr. Diaz went on a business trip, the odometer on his car showed 27274.9 kilometers. After his trip it showed 28109.4 kilometers. How many kilometers did he drive? _____

9 At a track meet Dan ran a race in 13.05 seconds, and Ken ran it in 11.48 seconds. How many seconds faster was Ken's time? _____

10 Marty received $100 for his birthday. He bought a bike for $79.99 and a CD for $11.49. How much does Marty have left? _____

Name_____

Every month Mrs. Joyner gets a statement from her bank. The statement for May showed she had $321.46 in her account on May 4 and $159.36 at the end of the month. This did not agree with her records.

Look at Mrs. Joyner's checkbook. Did she make an error in her calculations? If she did, correct the error so that her records show the same balance at the end of the month as the statement shows.

NUMBER	DATE	DESCRIPTION OF TRANSACTION	PAYMENT	DEPOSIT	BALANCE $ 321.46
211	May 5	Roger's Jewelers	−179. 35	$	−179.35 / 142.11
212	May 11	Carson's Fashions	−42. 37		−42.37 / 184.48
213	May 17	Lander's Service Station	−68. 23		−68.23 / 116.25
214	May 22	Noteworthy News	−22. 15		−22.15 / 94.10
	May 24	deposit		+150. 00	+150.00 / 244.10

Name_____

Multiply.

1 1.8
× 6

2 3.04
× 5

3 7.18
× 7

4 2.83
× 3

5 2.19
× 2

6 9.4
× 8

7 4.12
× 6

8 5.45
× 5

9 6.9
× 9

10 4.74
× 4

11 4.003
× 12

12 1.07
× 24

13 8.14
× 27

14 4.5
× 16

15 2.4
× 41

16 3.18
× 36

17 7.4
× 34

18 9.2
× 57

19 2.64
× 29

20 3.80
× 63

21 4.21
× 311

22 9.75
× 406

23 6.02
× 832

24 3.21
× 645

25 1.72
× 98

Solve these problems.

26 Marvin buys 312 pencils. Each pencil costs 16¢. How much
will the pencils cost?

_____

27 Janice buys eight packages of party favors. Each package
costs $2.79. Janice has $20. Does she have enough money?

_____

28 Joshua needs five shirts for school. Each shirt costs $12.75.
Will the shirts cost more than $65?

_____

In each problem two of the answers are clearly wrong and one is correct. Choose the correct answer.

1 $6 \times 2.3 =$ _____   **a.** 10.6   **b.** 13.8   **c.** 3.4

2 $5 \times 1.7 =$ _____   **a.** 4.5   **b.** 12.5   **c.** 8.5

3 $3.4 \times 8 =$ _____   **a.** 22.0   **b.** 27.2   **c.** 41.4

4 $0.9 \times 9 =$ _____   **a.** 8.1   **b.** 81   **c.** 0.81

5 $3 \times 0.43 =$ _____   **a.** 1.29   **b.** 3.71   **c.** 6.83

6 $4.6 \times 4 =$ _____   **a.** 192   **b.** 18.4   **c.** 1.62

7 $9.13 \times 5 =$ _____   **a.** 456.5   **b.** 4.565   **c.** 45.65

8 $0.02 \times 8 =$ _____   **a.** 0.16   **b.** 2.18   **c.** 16.02

9 $60 \times 41.4 =$ _____   **a.** 54.94   **b.** 347.4   **c.** 2484.0

10 $7.6 \times 14 =$ _____   **a.** 106.4   **b.** 100.64   **c.** 10,064

11 Use the function rule x —$\times 2$→ n —$+1$→ y to complete this chart.

x	1.1	2.1	3.1	4.1	5.1
y	3.2	5.2			

12 Plot the points on the graph.

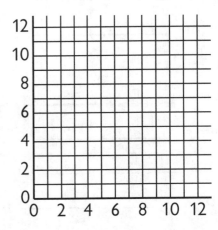

13 Do the five points seem to be on the same straight line?   _____

Name_____

Solve.

Remember: 1 kg = 1000 g.

1 4 g = _____ kg

2 65 g = _____ kg

3 70 g = _____ kg

4 280 g = _____ kg

5 921 g = _____ kg

6 3 g = _____ kg

7 6 kg = _____ g

8 0.1 kg = _____ g

9 41 kg = _____ g

10 0.007 kg = _____ g

Remember: 1000 mL = 1 L, and 1 mL = 0.001 L.

11 7 mL = _____ L

12 28 mL = _____ L

13 80 mL = _____ L

14 206 mL = _____ L

15 900 mL = _____ L

16 0.003 L = _____ mL

17 0.04 L = _____ mL

18 6 L = _____ mL

19 0.725 L = _____ mL

20 4.6 L = _____ mL

21 10 g = _____ kg

22 0.5 kg = _____ g

23 3500 m = _____ km

24 0.3 km = _____ m

25 3 km = _____ m

26 70 m = _____ km

27 125 g = _____ kg

28 0.25 kg = _____ g

29 660 m = _____ km

30 10 kg = _____ g

31 1.5 m = _____ mm

32 0.5 L = _____ mL

33 7500 mm = _____ m

34 375 mL = _____ L

35 850 mm = _____ m

36 6.2 L = _____ mL

37 11.4 m = _____ mm

38 0.8 L = _____ mL

Name_____

Find the volume of each box in cubic centimeters by figuring out how many cubes there are. Each cube is one cubic centimeter.

1 _____

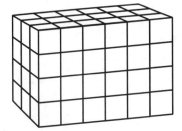

2 _____

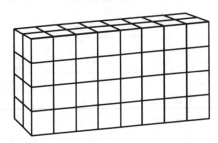

3 _____

4 _____

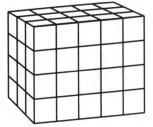

 **Solve these problems.**

5 Which is a better buy—a 1.8-liter bottle of tomato juice
for $1.29 or three 500-milliliter bottles of the same juice
for $0.45 each?   _____

6 Steven is making a batch of cookies. He has a recipe that
makes two dozen cookies but wants to make six dozen.
The recipe calls for 250 grams of sugar. How much sugar
should he use to make six dozen cookies?   _____

Multiply or divide.

1 $1000 \times 25.62 =$ _____

2 $1,000,000 \times 4.2931 =$ _____

3 $10 \times 3.85 =$ _____

4 $34.61 \div 100 =$ _____

5 $10,000 \times 35.9801 =$ _____

6 $42.34 \times 10 =$ _____

7 $476.12 \div 1000 =$ _____

8 $31.8872 \div 10,000 =$ _____

Multiply.

9 $34.1 \times 7 =$ _____

10 $1.305 \times 5208 =$ _____

11 $54.27 \times 74 =$ _____

12 $25.81 \times 9 =$ _____

13 $70.2 \times 45 =$ _____

14 $38 \times 12.7 =$ _____

Solve these problems.

15 Mrs. Ming was baking a cake. She needed $1\frac{3}{4}$ cups sugar for the cake and $2\frac{1}{2}$ cups sugar for the frosting. How much sugar did she need all together?   _____

16 Marco walked $1\frac{3}{8}$ miles from his friend's house. How many miles will Marco walk if he walks to his friend's house and back home?   _____

17 Mr. Hayden bought $3\frac{1}{2}$ feet of rope. He cut off a piece $1\frac{1}{3}$ feet long. How long was the remaining piece of rope?   _____

Name_____

Add or subtract.

1 1.45 + 6.92 = _____

2 0.04 + 5.83 = _____

3 75.408 – 13.716 = _____

4 40.34 + 23.67 = _____

5 12.78 – 3.89 = _____

6 5.3 – 2.8 = _____

Multiply or divide.

7 10,000 × 45.702 = _____

8 5.23 × 10 = _____

9 76.2309 ÷ 1000 = _____

10 125.06 ÷ 10 = _____

11 1,000,000 × 8.28076 = _____

12 10,000 ÷ 100 = _____

Multiply.

13 6.24 × 400 = _____

14 2.915 × 8 = _____

15 6 × 0.109 = _____

16 48.27 × 3 = _____

17 5 × 0.067 = _____

18 70 × 4.38 = _____

Add or subtract. Write your answer as a whole number, if possible, or as a mixed number or proper fraction reduced to lowest terms.

19 $\frac{2}{3} + 3\frac{1}{3} =$ _____

20 $7\frac{1}{16} + 2\frac{1}{4} =$ _____

21 $4\frac{1}{2} + 1\frac{3}{10} =$ _____

22 $4\frac{1}{2} - 1\frac{3}{10} =$ _____

23 $3\frac{3}{8} - 1\frac{3}{16} =$ _____

24 $3\frac{3}{8} + 1\frac{3}{16} =$ _____

Name_____

Draw <, >, or = to make each statement true.

1 0.345 ◯ 0.340   **2** 0.23 ◯ 0.023   **3** 0.004 ◯ 0.4

4 0.01 ◯ 0.010   **5** 0.75 ◯ 0.70   **6** 0.412 ◯ 0.634

7 0.8 ◯ 0.88   **8** 0.35 ◯ 0.04   **9** 0.9 ◯ 0.83

Find the value of the missing number.

1 meter = 10 decimeters = 100 centimeters = 1000 millimeters
1 m = 10 dm = 100 cm = 1000 mm

10 _____ dm = 4 m   **11** 1 dm = _____ mm

12 200 cm = _____ m   **13** 50 dm = _____ m

14 _____ dm = 300 mm   **15** 2 dm, 6 cm, 7 mm = _____ m

16 9 dm, 4 mm = _____ m   **17** 38 m = _____ mm

Draw a circle. Then shade the appropriate fraction.

18 Shade $\frac{3}{6}$ of it. Then shade another $\frac{1}{6}$ of it.

19 Shade $\frac{2}{3}$ of it.